Flying Concorde

Brian Calvert was born in 1933 in China (where his family was later interned by the Japanese during the Second World War) and educated at Stowe School, Buckinghamshire. He joined BOAC (now part of British Airways) in 1957, after National Service in the Fleet Air Arm. For his first two years with the airline he flew as a navigator, and this led to a lifelong interest in the subject. He is now a Fellow of the Royal Institute of Navigation.

He has taken part in a fascinating period of aviation history, flying such famous civil aircraft as Boeing Stratocruisers, Britannias, Comet IVs and VC-10s, as well as Concorde. In 1966 he joined the airline's Flight Development unit, where he became closely involved with the introduction of new aircraft and flight systems, and where his interpretations of the needs of aircrew had a significant influence on aircraft design. For his work in this field, and on the introduction and trials of new navigation systems, he received the Airlines Avionics Institute's Volare Award.

During Concorde's entry into service, as Flight Manager (Technical), he was responsible for deciding on the methods by which Concorde would be flown, the flying qualities of the aircraft and the suitability of potential routes, and played an active role in complicated and protracted negotiations with foreign governments (including that of the USA). He carried out acceptance trials on the new aircraft and flew several of its inaugural flights. In 1977 he received the Guild of Air Pilots and Navigators' Brackley Trophy, and in 1979 was awarded the Queen's Commendation for Valuable Services in the Air.

Brian Calvert is married to the writer and games inventor Mary Danby and has three children. He lives in an eighteenth-century cottage in West Berkshire, and his spare-time interests include navigation, opera and boating on the River Thames. He left British Airways in 1982, soon after this book was written, to pursue a second career in business aviation. He now works for Field Aviation Ltd at Heathrow Airport, where he often watches Concorde take off past his office window.

Flying Concorde

Brian Calvert

Airlife
England

629. 13334 9/01522115

This edition published in 1989 by Airlife Publishing Ltd
Reprinted 1995, 1998

First published by
Airlife Publishing Ltd in association with
Fontana Paperbacks 1981

ISBN 1 85310 027 7

Printed in England by Livesey Ltd, Shrewsbury.

Airlife Publishing Ltd

101 Longden Road, Shrewsbury SY3 9EB, England

'It seems that perfection is achieved not when there is nothing more to add, but when there is nothing more to take away.'

Antoine de Saint Exupery, *Terre des Hommes*

Contents

Foreword

Concorde is a remarkable aeroplane. Although its military relations have for many years flown at twice the speed of sound – and even faster – none of them can match Concorde's unique feature: the length of time it can sustain supersonic speeds without in-flight refuelling.

Just how and why this is possible, and the problems and battles which had to be overcome, are part of Concorde's fascinating story.

But from the airline point of view, Concorde had to be just another aeroplane, maintained and operated by ordinary airline personnel. The period from the early days of the first prototype to the inaugural passenger service in 1976 was a difficult one, made more so by the initial lack of firm customers. And the fact that too many people regarded the concept of a supersonic airliner as being a good excuse to start with a fresh piece of paper on everything perhaps made more work than would otherwise have been necessary. The transformation of Concorde into a practical airliner was the result of a great deal of effort on the part of various people and organizations. No one made a greater contribution than Brian Calvert, particularly in navigational techniques and operational procedures.

Flying Concorde is written in a manner which gives anyone who knows the author as well as I do a feeling of talking to him in person. He knows the aeroplane, and he writes about it in such a way that even the most technical aspects can be readily understood. It is a delight to read.

The story of Concorde is a large subject, concerning as it does both the technological history of the aircraft and its struggle to be accepted as an airliner. I am sure that all those who read this book will enjoy it as much as I have and will observe the considerable modesty of the author.

BRIAN TRUBSHAW
Director of Flight Test, British Aerospace

Acknowledgments

A book of this kind cannot be written without help from many people. Those from British Aerospace who have given generously of their time and knowledge include Norman Barfield, Howard Berry, F. G. Clarke, Leo Schafer, Dick Thornborough and Brian Trubshaw. I am grateful also to the directors of British Airways for allowing me to write the book, and for not asking for anything to be taken out. Of my present and former colleagues, Tom Craft, Gordon Davidson, Dudley Foy, Tony Meadows, Brian Walpole and Ron Wilson were particularly able to help.

I am indebted for assistance in researching photographs to Ted Ashman of British Aerospace, Bill Oliver of British Airways, Arthur Falkowitz and Arthur Gibson.

Finally, I should like to thank my wife who, a professional in these matters, taught me a great deal about how to write as I went along.

Photographs are reproduced by permission of British Aerospace (3, 4, 6, 10, 13, 14, 16), British Airways (2, 7, 18, 19), Arthur Falkowitz (20, 21, 22, 23, 24, 25), Arthur Gibson (1), Alison Lornie (5), Central Press Photos (8, 11, 15) and Syndication International (9, 12, 17). All colour photographs are by courtesy of British Airways.

PART I
The Airliner

1. Encounters

'How do you like your coffee, Captain – cream and sugar?'

We are at Thirty West, the half-way point between the European and North American continents, and the stewardess in charge of the forward galley is looking after her aircrew during a pause in serving the passengers' meals.

Mach 2. On autopilot, 11 miles high, moving at 23 miles a minute. Nearly twice as high as Mount Everest, faster than a rifle bullet leaving its barrel. The side windows are hot to the touch, from the friction of the passing air. Despite the speed, we can talk without raising our voices.

'Milk, please, and no sugar.'

Through the windscreen, between the sloping bars of the transparent visor, the horizon 300 miles away is whitish and indistinct – an oblique view of the tops of the clouds ahead. Nevertheless the earth's curvature is detectable. As the eye travels down towards the sea, the clouds appear to form up into the familiar patterns of North Atlantic weather: a series of anticlockwise swirls of low pressure, with warm and cold fronts spoking out from them. Patches of unstable air lie between, scattered with thunder-clouds which, when seen from so far above, look surprisingly benign. That's what Britain will be getting, the day after tomorrow.

Upwards from the horizon, the sky darkens, becoming space-purple above – pure colour, with nothing for the eye to focus on. There is no sense of movement. No rushing of air. No turbulence. We seem to be stopped, fixed in the stratosphere, while the earth rotates beneath. Magical. Somewhere in the back of the mind lurks the wish that this was really so, that we didn't have to come down again – but there is work to do, and the three white-shirted figures on the flight deck get on with it.

No zippered flying suits here, no bulbous helmets, no terse commands. Calm and unhurried, the two pilots and the flight engineer are quietly busy, attending to the aeroplane: scanning the instruments, programming the flight path, assessing the remaining fuel and range, checking each other's actions. The coffee, moving a mile every 2·7 seconds, doesn't even ripple.

Flying Concorde seems so normal now that it comes as something of a surprise to recall how startling it all seemed at first, how like something from science fiction. . . .

11 December 1967 was a bright but bitterly cold day at Toulouse, where 001 had been built. A tiered stand faced the hangar whose closed doors, like the curtains of a vast proscenium, hid the first prototype: not yet ready for flight, but complete enough for the roll-out ceremony we were about to see. A chilled military band was assembled in front of the building, tooting an occasional tune. As one of the crew of a VC10 which had flown BOAC's board members in, I found myself seated towards the back, among a group of stewardesses from the many airlines who had taken options on the aircraft. Some of the girls, with the practicality of their occupation, had brought rugs. The band struggled thinly through a final number and marched off.

The hangar doors rolled back, accompanied by the usual warning whistles . . . and there she was, sideways on, long, sharp and sleek. The shuffling and foot-stamping died out, and a long silence followed as the crowd took it all in. There had been photographs, of course, but this, the first sight of a real Concorde, stopped the breath, leaving it hanging in condensed wisps around the thousand-odd heads.

After several seconds clapping started. As if cued by the applause, an immaculately overalled mechanic appeared from stage right, walked across to the bright yellow tug which was attached to the nosewheel, paused to draw on a pair of smart leather gloves and climbed up into the driving seat. With Gallic elegance, he shot his cuffs before reaching forward to start the engine. Clapping broke out again, and laughter for this man's sense of drama. He towed 001 out slowly, in a wide arc, to reverse its direction and park it with its right side facing the stand. As the aeroplane moved around its half-circle we saw for the first time how the extraordinary shape seemed to change as different angles were presented. The nose at one point appeared to swing almost over the crowd. As its shadow passed my section, an 'Aaah!' of appreciation escaped from the group of stewardesses. I thought then: 'Who wouldn't want to be a Concorde pilot?'

I had joined BOAC's Flight Development Department a few months earlier. The job involved studying new aeroplanes, new flight decks, instruments, automatic landing equipment, navigation systems – anything to do with the business of flying new aircraft or improving old ones. It was a particularly exciting time. The Boeing 747 was being designed, and with it were coming advances in technology which were a direct result of the US space programme. Two supersonic transports, Concorde and the US SST, were making progress as well – the first was now a reality but some way from flying, the second still very much a 'paper' aeroplane.

The 747, which would arrive before the SSTs, posed two principal challenges: it was more than twice the size of its predecessors, and it would be the first of the new generation of heavily automated aircraft. Both of these features demanded a good deal of adaptation from aircrew and airports, but at least the changes would be made against the background of the well-tried family of Boeing designs. Concorde, on the other hand, was going to be a whole new *kind* of aircraft, flying at speeds and heights known only to a select group of military pilots – fit young men in pressure suits. The challenge here was to make this extraordinary machine, this visitor from the future, into an airliner.

After that first meeting in Toulouse, my contact with the aeroplane was, to start with, tenuous. BOAC had not yet decided to order. But whether or not we would eventually buy the aircraft (and firm orders were not, in fact, placed until 1972), the airline needed to be properly prepared. A series of studies was carried out, on payload and range, on the supersonic boom, on weather in the upper atmosphere, on air traffic control. For a full year, sample flight plans were made out daily, using actual winds and temperatures. This trial confirmed that a fixed route structure could be used over the North Atlantic, whereas subsonic aircraft needed to vary their routes in order to find the most favourable winds. A BOAC flight engineer, John Lidiard, was assigned to fly on some test flights, to gain experience of the systems in actual use. From Air France, Commandant Pierre

Dudal was detached to fly with the test team.

Gradually, the airlines gained knowledge and experience; gradually, the aeroplane was being transformed into an airliner. In 1974 I was asked to join the management of the Concorde project in what had become, by then, British Airways. It took some thinking about. On the one hand, it was by no means certain that supersonic flying would be commercially successful – it would obviously be an expensive form of travel, and there was a clear trend towards larger, more economical aircraft. A division of opinion existed within the airline management: there were still senior people who hoped, believed, even, that it would somehow go away – and it seldom pays, in career terms, to tie oneself to a project which does not have the wholehearted support of those above.

On the other hand, it was becoming a superb machine. It would be immensely exciting to fly. It clearly worked. And it was under attack from nearly every quarter. It is a little hard to remember, now, just how strident the campaign against Concorde in most of the British and American press had become. There was every reason why laxity in the control of government spending should be attacked, and people were becoming properly concerned to preserve their environment, but why on earth was it necessary for journalists, politicians, even scientists to lie so much? Where they did not lie, they distorted. Where they did not distort, they used the words 'may cause . . .' to implant the idea of yet another horror.

Then there was the appalling cycle of British post-war aviation to consider – a long series of grandiose projects, begun with fanfares by one government, and cancelled, amid recriminations, by a successor. It seemed about time that one project, at least, was carried through. It seemed right that, for once, the British public should be allowed to see for itself what had been bought with all the money spent on its behalf. For all these reasons, I took the job.

The aircraft was by then doing hot weather trials in the Arabian Gulf, where the first British Airways pilots and flight engineers joined the test crews as observers. I flew out to Dubai in August 1974. A few days later, by which time we were based in Singapore, I got my hands on the controls for the first time. I shall never forget those first impressions, formed after I had climbed into the left-hand seat, off the east coast of Malaysia. It seemed as if the aeroplane had been built simply to delight me. The springy, responsive feel of the controls, the long nose pointing ahead, the enormous power available at a quick shift of the forearm, the stability, the precision . . . all brought back the excitement I had felt when, as a young National Service pilot in the RNVR, I flew my first fighter, the Seafire XVII – although nearly half the history of aviation separated the two aircraft.

This first impression of Concorde's liveliness, almost of its being alive, has persisted. It was obvious from the beginning that a few features would take some getting used to: the 'dragginess' of the delta wing at high angles of attack, the peculiar attitude on final approach, the rather odd landing technique and the sheer speed at which the normal events of flying took place. But the simple physical pleasure of flying the aeroplane, once experienced, made it all seem possible, and very attractive.

Over the intervening years, some of the novelty has gone, but none of the pleasure. Concorde still looks marvellous, still responds like a well-schooled racehorse, is still unique.

2. The Aeroplane

There is no doubt that Concorde is the most beautiful aeroplane. Flying overhead at a few thousand feet it is slender, fem-
inine, dart-like. On final approach it suggests a bird coming in
to land. Just after landing, with its nose still down, it might be
some prehistoric monster with curious eating habits. On the
ground, from under the nose, it is four square engine bays slung
from minute wings. After years, now, of looking at it from
every possible angle I am still not sure I can pin down its shape
in my mind. It seems constantly to change, to assume new
forms. This is perhaps one reason why, wherever it goes, it still
turns heads and stops traffic. Its visual appeal exists quite separ-
ately from its function. Yet function dictated every line, every
twist in the wing, the stalky nose-leg, the pointed, drooping
nose.

The Wing

Every airliner's wing-shape is an aerodynamic compromise.
Over the last twenty years or so cruising speeds have increased
from about 300 mph (propeller aircraft) to 600 mph (subsonic
jets) and finally to 1300 mph (Mach 2 SSTs – supersonic transports). The effect of this shows clearly in their wings: as speed
has increased, so has the degree of sweepback.

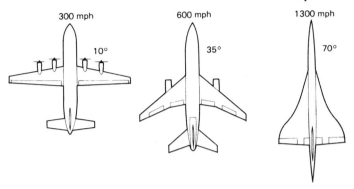

Sweepback

The wing section has changed, too: it has become thinner in relation to its chord.

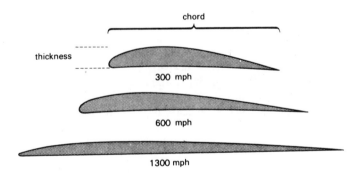

Thickness

So has the aspect ratio (the relationship of span to mean chord).

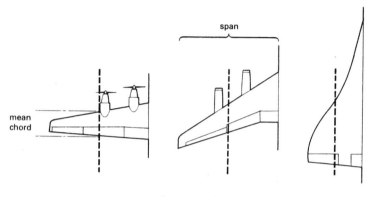

Aspect ratio

There are good aerodynamic explanations for all these changes, but they are also obvious to the eye – the faster an aeroplane goes, the more dart-shaped it becomes.

The choices open to an aircraft designer are, of course, by no means as simple as this. The wing must be strong enough to support the weight of the body and engines, and to survive gusts at high speed. It must have enough room in it to carry most of the fuel, and to enclose at least part of the landing gear when retracted. Finally, and most importantly, it must be able to provide enough lift in slow-speed flight to allow it to take off and land at airports, where space is limited.

While cruising speeds have increased more than fourfold, landing speeds have increased by only half: from about 120 mph to 180 mph. As a result, the range of speeds over which wings have to be effective has grown enormously, wing design becoming proportionately more ingenious. Here a little explanation of how a wing works is needed (for those to whom the subject isn't old hat). A wing exists to support the weight of the aircraft to which it is attached, and depends on motion to generate the lift. Air passing over it moves further and faster, and as a result reduces in pressure compared with the air beneath. This generates a sucking effect, which is lift. The greater the speed, the more lift a wing produces.

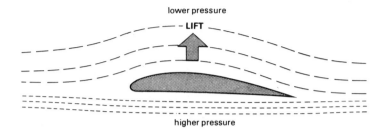

lower pressure

LIFT

higher pressure

Lift

Propeller aircraft, operating over a speed range of 200 mph or so, needed a little help at low speed, so flaps were attached. These altered the camber of the wing and thus increased the pressure difference (and therefore lift) when the aircraft were flying slowly.

camber (normal)

flap

camber (flaps down)

Camber – with and without flaps

When wings were swept back to about 30 degrees for the jet transport, the slow-speed efficiency deteriorated, so improvements were made to the flaps, and (mainly to smooth the airflow) slats were added to the leading edge.

The most exciting moment of a flight on, say, a Jumbo is the preparation for landing. Each wing sprouts slats from its leading edge and, over several minutes, flaps pour out of the back like a series of mini-wings, seeming almost to double its area and camber. Modern flaps are marvellous pieces of mechanical engineering and worth watching in action.

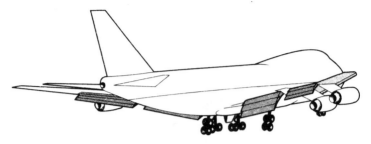

Slats and flaps

Concorde's wing has none of this: the weight and drag penalty in the cruise would be too great. On the other hand, its wing is not just heavily swept back; it is a slender delta shape overall, with a double-curved leading edge. It twists and droops as well, making the apparently simple shape complex in detail.

Twist and droop

The slender delta has a characteristic not found in other wing shapes. It can fly successfully, producing enough lift, at a wide range of angles of attack to the airflow – up to angles well above those which would cause other wings to stall (the breakaway of the airflow which causes almost complete loss of lift). This allows Concorde to cope with its wide speed-range simply by changing its angle of attack, rather as a bird does. The built-in

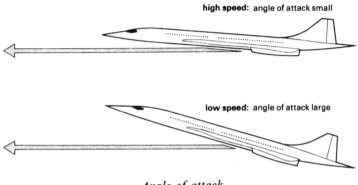

Angle of attack

ability to increase its lift at high angles of attack enables the slender delta to delay the stall. The mechanism which produces this happy effect is called vortex lift.

All swept wings create vortices (swirls of air) at their tips. These can be seen on humid days as twin trails of vapour coming off the wingtips of airliners coming in to land or taking off. The delta wing, however, as its angle of attack increases (at slower speeds), creates larger, slower moving vortices which creep forward along the leading edge, eventually enveloping the whole upper surface of the wing, thus further increasing the suction and therefore the lift.

Watch a Concorde take off on a really soggy day, and you will see it half-disappear into a cloud of its own making, as the reduction in pressure forces the water vapour suspended in the air to condense.

Vortex lift (which, incidentally, because of its slow rate of rotation, is not especially severe in its effect on following aircraft) is fundamental to Concorde's ability to fly slowly. It also produces one of the characteristic qualities of the feel of Concorde to a passenger. The air swirling over the wing at slow speeds produces a bouncing motion, at a frequency of about half a second, which is sometimes mistaken for light turbulence. The motion disappears quickly as soon as speed is increased after take-off, but is there throughout the final approach.

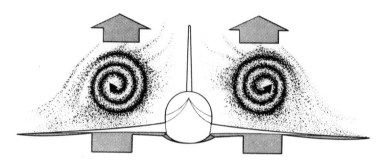

Vortex lift

Concorde's wing, then, makes sense. There are compelling reasons which dictated all its features, many of which are in various degrees different from those of other airliners. They all stem from the extraordinary range of speeds at which Concorde has to be able to fly: from its ability to take off from Heathrow in the morning rush-hour, cross the Atlantic at Mach 2, gracefully slow down to join the traffic flow into Kennedy airport and land in sequence with all the other aircraft.

The Flying Controls

Stick and rudder pedals – Orville and Wilbur Wright used them on 17 December 1903 to steer their fragile craft through the first controlled flight of a powered aircraft. These same controls have been employed in one form or another ever since. The simple stick, held in one hand, is used by the pilot to pitch the aeroplane up or down, and to roll it to the right or left. The pilot's feet, resting on the pedals, usually move in sympathy with the left/right movements of the hand.

The stick has grown somewhat since then, separating the two functions of pitch and roll, so that on a modern airliner you will find what the makers call a control column (also known as a 'handwheel' or a 'yoke'), though many pilots still refer to it

Stick and rudder

simply as 'the stick'. This is really a vestigial wheel mounted on a hinged column. It is open at the top because a complete wheel

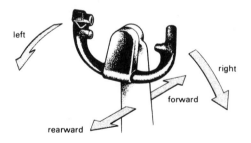

Control column

would obscure some of the instruments and is anyway un-necessary: the wheel never needs to be turned through more than 90 degrees, and one hand can usually do it.

maximum left roll

Control wheel movement

The apparent similarity between this and the steering wheel of a car is deceptive. An aeroplane's wheel is normally in the neutral position during a turn: a car's is certainly not. Moving a car's wheel selects a particular angle for the front wheels, and therefore the rate at which you want to turn. Moving an aircraft's wheel selects a particular deflection of the ailerons and

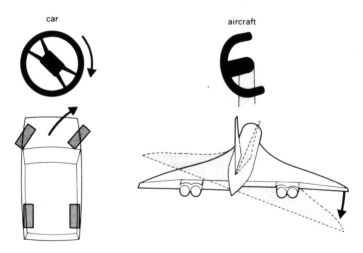

car

aircraft

Starting a turn

therefore the rate at which you want to apply roll – a very different process. A car driver holds the wheel over throughout a turn, but once an aircraft has reached the required bank angle, the wheel is returned to neutral.

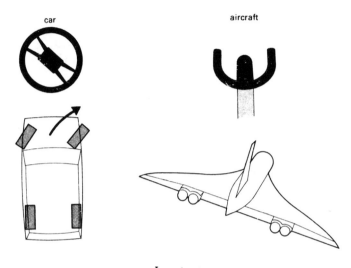

In a turn

It is the bank angle which causes the aeroplane to turn, and when the turn is complete the wheel has to be moved in the opposite direction to roll the bank off. Once the wings are level the wheel is centred again.

A car set up to behave like this would be rather too exciting to drive (imagine starting a turn and then needing to move the steering wheel in the opposite direction to stop the turn tightening up), but it works very well in the air.

Just why these differences exist is a question of some interest. It is probable that car steering followed the methods used with horses and ships. A carriage is turned right by pulling on the right rein, and the pressure is held until the horse has turned far enough. A ship's wheel or tiller is also held over during a turn. A break was necessary in this historical pattern of control when aircraft arrived, simply because banking was the only efficient means of changing direction. But there is a good reason why this system continues – an aircraft stays in a turn much longer.

It takes a full minute to reverse course at normal rates. At Mach 2 the same change takes about twelve minutes. Clearly, holding the wheel over for these periods would be unpleasant.

Concorde's control column works in exactly the same way as any other airliner's, but it looks rather different. Again pitch and roll are separated, but the wheel is replaced by a 'ramshorn', which moves through only 60 degrees each way.

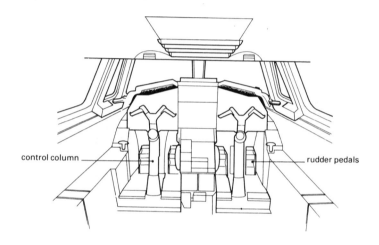

control column   rudder pedals

Concorde's controls

It looks rather awkward, and when the airlines' pilots first saw the design there was an almost universal cry of dismay. Some of us half-suspected they were a job lot left over from the production line of the Bristol Britannia, which was one of the few aeroplanes to be fitted with this kind of control. They were not, of course – the ramshorn shape particularly suits the narrowness of the cockpit, allowing full movement left and right over the pilot's legs, and giving a good view of the mass of instruments in front of it. In practice, pilots quickly adapted to it, even finding some advantage in the slightly more natural motion when only one hand is being used.

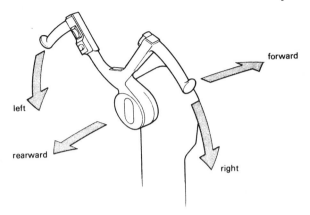

Ramshorn

Whatever shape they are, all the flying controls on any flight deck are designed to move parts of the aeroplane in order to change its direction. Most aircraft have three types of control surfaces: elevators, ailerons and rudders. These surfaces provide control in pitch, roll and yaw.

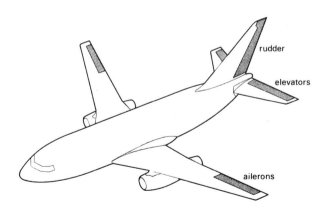

Control surfaces

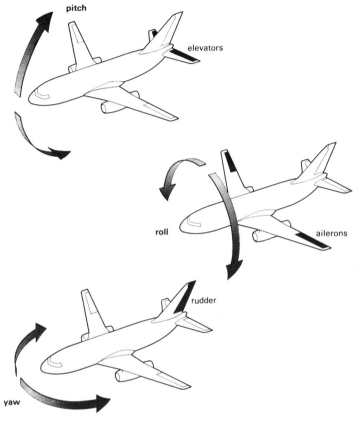

Pitch, roll and yaw

Concorde's rudder, like that of most swept-wing aircraft, is used mostly for balancing purposes. It is mounted, in the normal way, on the tail fin. There is no tailplane on which to mount elevators but the wing's chord is so long that control surfaces fitted to the trailing edge of the wing can do the jobs both of elevators and of ailerons. Because of their dual purpose, these control surfaces have acquired the amalgamated name 'elevons'.

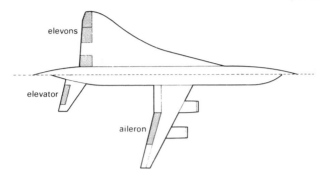

Elevons

In pitch the elevons all work together: in roll the two sides move in opposite directions.

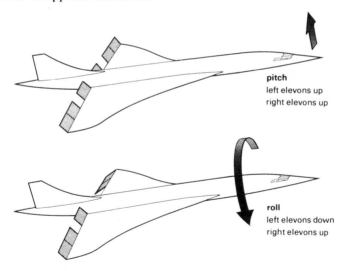

pitch
left elevons up
right elevons up

roll
left elevons down
right elevons up

Pitch and roll

The signals for roll and pitch are mixed together so that when, say, pitch up and roll right are required at the same time, the elevons move appropriately in combination.

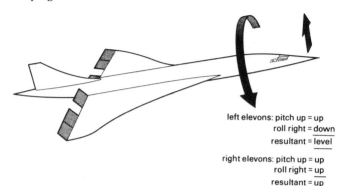

left elevons: pitch up = up
roll right = down
resultant = level

right elevons: pitch up = up
roll right = up
resultant = up

Pitch and roll together

The pilot does not move the elevons and rudder himself – the forces involved are far too great. Between the control column and the moving surfaces there needs to be a system of motive power and a method of controlling that power, rather in the same way as the muscular and nervous systems of the human body move our limbs.

The 'muscles' which move the control surfaces are called Power Flying Control Units. There are three under each wing

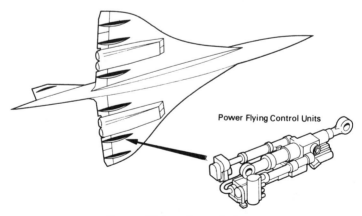

Power Flying Control Units

Power Flying Control Units

and two on the tail fin, each independently powering one of the eight control surfaces.

To do the work, the units are fed with hydraulic fluid, pressurized to 4000 pounds per square inch by engine-driven pumps (which, incidentally, is why a parked Concorde usually has its elevons hanging down – the power is off, and gravity has taken over). There are three separate hydraulic systems, which do a number of jobs, including raising and lowering the wheels. Two of these permanently power the flying controls, and the third is available at any time for back-up purposes.

The 'nerves' of the flying control system, which translate the pilot's movements into action, are of great importance to the safety and even the comfort of the aeroplane, so there are three of these 'signalling channels' as well. The main and standby systems are electrical: shifts of the control column or rudder pedals are felt by sensors and transmitted along wires to the control

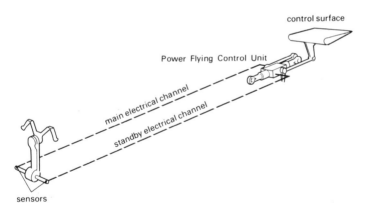

Electrical signalling

units. These channels use special power-packs which produce their own current at a frequency designed to resist interference. The third system is mechanical, linking the control column, through a hydraulic relay jack, directly to the control units.

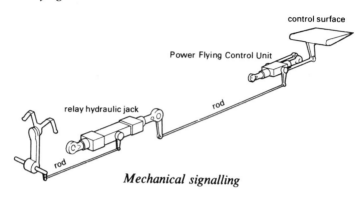

Mechanical signalling

These three methods of signalling provide plenty of spare capacity: the mechanical channel has never had to be used in five years of service. However, there is yet another method of moving the control surfaces, designed for the unlikely case that the column itself might be partially or wholly jammed. Should this happen, strain gauges can measure the actual forces being applied by the pilot and transmit them electrically, through the normal circuits.

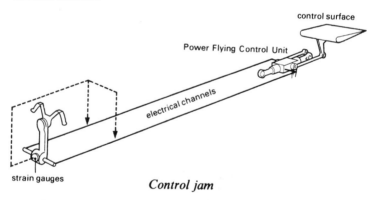

Control jam

Electrical signalling (or fly-by-wire, as it is sometimes known) is unusual in civil aircraft, but it is responsible for many of the features which make Concorde so pleasant to fly. It provides the ability to interpose between the pilot and the controls further signals which refine the aircraft's flying qualities. The first of these is auto-stabilisation, which acts in all three axes (pitch, roll and yaw) to improve the aircraft's natural stability, and to smooth out turbulence. It will also apply some rudder control if an engine fails, to counteract the resulting yaw. A second electronic box, the Safety Flight System, provides protection against accidentally reaching too high an angle of attack (the equivalent of approaching the stall on other aircraft), first by gently opposing the pilot's demand, then by shaking the stick (accompanied by a loud rattling noise) and finally by wobbling it quite viciously. Should the pilot be so bent on disaster that he ignores all of these progressively more insistent messages, the system, despairing of his sanity, will put all the elevons firmly down, to decrease the angle of attack and regain a safe flying speed.

Another circuit in the control lines protects against control reversal. Those who remember the film *The Sound Barrier* may

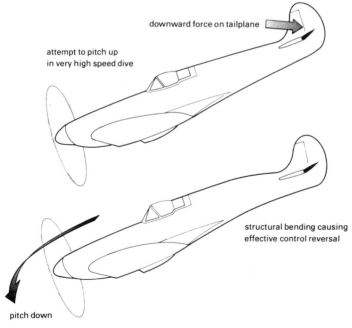

downward force on tailplane

attempt to pitch up
in very high speed dive

structural bending causing
effective control reversal

pitch down

Aeroelasticity

wonder how the phenomenon which formed the core of the story was overcome. Second World War fighter aircraft, when dived well beyond their design speeds, tended to bend when the control surfaces were moved, because of the very high loads involved. As a result, the pilot's control demands could be neutralized, or sometimes reversed. The more advanced design of Concorde's structure makes it much more resistant to these distorting forces; the electrical signalling helps, too. If the aircraft gets substantially above its design speed, the outboard elevons (on the thinnest section of the wing) are automatically neutralized, so that no twisting is possible. The work of pitching the aeroplane up, to reduce the speed, is then done by the four inboard elevons, whose hinges are behind the most solid parts of the wings.

These are just some of the interventions made by 'thinking' electronic systems between the pilot's movements and the activity of the control surfaces. Enormous power is used, but it is modulated with great delicacy. A single example demonstrates the success of the end result: at Mach 2, Concorde can be flown with just two fingers.

Control surfaces have a second function: trim or balance. The rudder on modern aircraft is used chiefly for this purpose. Ailerons (or the roll function of the elevons in Concorde's case) are used in this way to compensate for any imbalance in the amount of fuel in each wing. Elevator, or pitch, trim is used most often of the three, on all aircraft, in response to aerodynamic shifts in the pattern of lift over the wing at different speeds.

Centre of Gravity and Fuel Transfer

Any swept wing, designed to fly close to Mach 1, experiences changes in the pressure pattern over it. These always have the effect of moving the centre of lift rearward as speed increases.

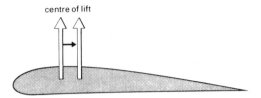

centre of lift

Effect of increasing Mach number

As a result there is a tendency to pitch down, and on subsonic aircraft this is trimmed out by an upward deflection of the elevators, or, more usually, by moving the tailplane itself, as this causes less drag.

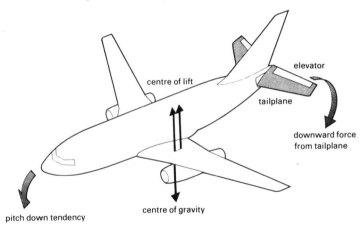

elevator

centre of lift

tailplane

downward force
from tailplane

pitch down tendency

centre of gravity

Trimming by tailplane

An aircraft flying at Mach 2 needs to do rather more, as the rearward movement of the centre of lift is much greater. Some of the effects of the aerodynamic changes are countered by the gentle cambers and twists of Concorde's wing, but there still remains a shift of about six feet to be accounted for. That may not sound much, but the force involved (the lift) is opposing, and therefore equal to, the weight – which may be 170 tons at the time.

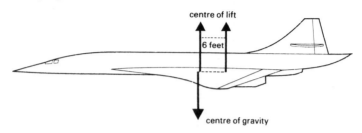

Trim change at Mach 2

Moving the elevons up to compensate for this would obviously produce an appalling increase in drag, and would leave precious little further upward deflection available for control purposes. Instead, fuel is moved to change the internal weight distribution. Most of Concorde's 95 tons of fuel is kept in tanks in the wings, but the forward two, and another in the tail cone, are used for trim as well as storage. Together they hold about 33 tons.

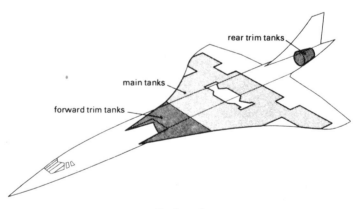

Fuel tanks

As acceleration towards Mach 1 begins, fuel is pumped out of the forward tanks to two destinations: the collector tanks in the wings and the rear trim tank.

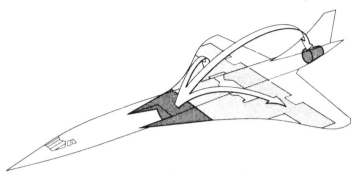

Fuel transfer (rearward)

During the flight, between take-off and Mach 2, around twenty tons of fuel are moved in this way, and the result is a rearward shift of six feet for the centre of gravity, neatly balancing the change in the centre of lift.

At the end of the cruise, when the aircraft is slowed down, the reverse happens.

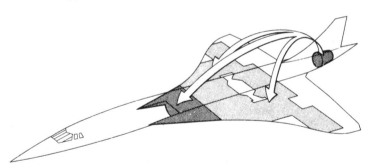

Fuel transfer (forward)

Concorde needs this system to achieve the necessary efficiency in high-speed flight, but it provides several extra benefits. The ability to put the aircraft's weight in the right place throughout the flight means that very little use need be made of pitch trim. This is a bonus for the pilot, for large trim changes are a nuisance, tending to make accurate flying difficult. Another bonus comes, oddly enough, from being able to put the aeroplane deliberately a little out of trim. On take-off and landing, the centre of gravity is placed slightly further back than it need be. As a result the elevons go down to counteract this rearward weight shift, and in doing so increase the camber of the wing. We have now come round full-circle to achieving the effect of flaps – producing more lift for the slow-speed portions of the flight – without the weight penalty of fitting any mechanical extensions to the wing.

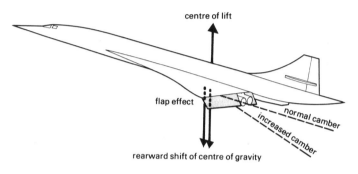

Flap effect

There is one further method of increasing the lift of a slender delta wing: the addition of canards, or foreplanes. The Soviet TU144 makes use of these, extending them for take-off and landing. They sprout from behind the flight deck, like ears.

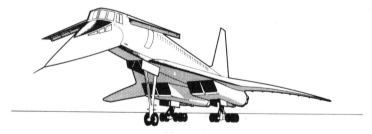

Canards (TU144)

These produce a little lift themselves, but, more importantly, they cause a tendency to pitch up which, when countered by down elevon, produces once more the desirable flap effect. Concorde can manage without canards, carrying only tiny foreplanes, known as 'moustaches', which are there principally to smooth the airflow over the innermost sections of the wing: those parts which get least benefit from vortex lift.

Concorde's fuel transfer system is in a real sense part of its flying controls. Although unseen, it produces the balanced state around which the elevons work and, when necessary, converts part of their function to improve low-speed performance.

When a pilot thinks of an aeroplane, he remembers not only what it looks like, but also what it is like to fly. What, then, makes an aeroplane attractive to handle? Attractiveness is very subjective, but most of the answer probably lies in the qualities of 'feel', response, trim and stability. A feel system replaces the natural forces a pilot would sense from unpowered controls in reply to his control movements, by feeding back to the control column a tactile sense of what he is asking the control surfaces to do. It needs to be as powerful as is necessary to prevent accidental or over-vigorous movements, but as light as possible to keep the muscular work to a minimum. Response, in this sense, means the aircraft's ability to produce rates of pitch or roll which are fast enough to meet the pilot's needs: an airliner does not, for example, need a fighter's rate of roll, but sluggish controls make a gusty approach very hard work. Trimming is a necessity, but the need for trim should not be sudden or severe. Stability is the tendency for an aeroplane to stay where it is put, and to recover from external disturbances. All modern airliners have good natural stability, but they vary in the speed with which disturbances are damped out. The best qualities of damping come largely from artificial electronic systems.

On all four counts Concorde scores highly. The feel is light, particularly in roll, the response is all it need be, the trim required is small and never sudden, and the stability is quite excellent.

The Undercarriage

The wing shape is responsible for the long undercarriage legs and the small pair of wheels under the tail. The high angle of attack on final approach leads to a pitch angle on touchdown of about 11 degrees. This puts the rearmost part of the engines nearest the ground, and the legs must be long enough to stop them touching. The tailwheels are a second line of defence, in case the touchdown angle turns out to be too high.

Landing attitude

Long undercarriage legs are no particular problem to a designer, but there has to be somewhere to put them when they are raised. The nosewheel simply retracts forward, but the main legs, which must fold inwards, have to shorten themselves before they reach their bays. Mechanical links inside the shock-absorber tubes pull them up as they swing into their raised position.

Undercarriage legs shortening

Raising the landing gear is, in fact, a series of events, all controlled by an electrical sequencing system:

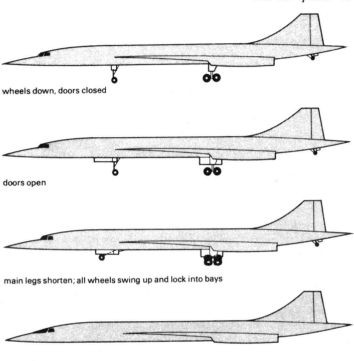

wheels down, doors closed

doors open

main legs shorten; all wheels swing up and lock into bays

doors close

Undercarriage raising

On lowering, the reverse happens: the doors open, the legs swing down, the main legs lengthen and lock into position, and the doors close around the extended legs.

The Brakes

On a typical landing – at a speed of about 170 mph – the exceptionally powerful brakes bring the 100-ton craft to a stop within about a mile. Their most demanding task is coping with a rejected take-off from the 'decision speed' (V_1), which can be up to about 190 mph at a weight of 185 tons.

Any moving object contains energy, and bringing it to a stop is a process of absorbing that energy. This is what all brakes, even a bicycle's, do. The amount of energy to be absorbed varies with the vehicle's mass (in this case equal to weight) and the square of its speed. So, surprisingly, stopping a Boeing 747, at twice the take-off weight but about 50 mph slower at V_1, requires the absorption of less energy than a Concorde.

The brakes that deal with this contain carbon discs, and are controlled by hinged toe-plates attached to the pilots' rudder pedals. Like the flying controls, the brakes are powered hydraulically and controlled by electrical signals from the toe-plates. An advanced anti-skid system modulates the braking pressures applied by the pilot.

A few expensive cars, and all modern airliners, are fitted with anti-skid systems – very valuable and essentially simple devices. A braked wheel skids when it has lost adhesion with the ground, usually because there is a thin layer of water or ice under it. When this happens, its rotation slows down abruptly and, if the brakes are kept on, stops altogether. An anti-skid system looks at this rate of slowing down and decides whether it is due to proper braking or to skidding. If the rate is faster than a certain 'reference' value, known to be outside possible braking rates, it will reduce the degree of braking until contact between wheel and ground is regained. The only crudity of this kind of system is that it has to use a fixed reference value, whereas the true maximum rate of slowing down increases as the vehicle's speed reduces. Concorde uses signals from its nosewheel (which is not braked and therefore does not skid) to vary the reference value so that the modulation of the brake pressure always happens close to the optimum at all speeds.

All pilots practise rejected take-offs in the simulator but in 1976, the first year of operation, we suffered from a rash of real ones. Most were caused by false warnings from a rather over-complicated monitoring system which could have been ignored, but a crew has no time to hold a committee meeting while thundering down a runway, so we became rather more practised than we need have been at this most irritating manoeuvre – irritating chiefly because up to an hour's delay may be needed to allow the brakes to cool. Absorbing the energy of a landing aircraft heats them up to about 300°C, but a rejected take-off, at a higher speed and weight, can cause the temperature to rise to over 500°C. Even the cooling fans fitted in each wheel take time to dissipate this amount of heat.

The Nose and Visor

The high angle of attack on landing dictates the need for a moveable nose – a fixed one would completely obscure the runway, as the available downward view to the pilot would be only about 5 degrees.

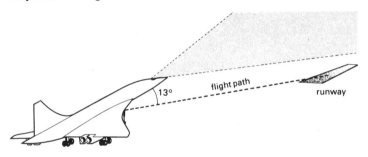

Runway view

So the nose, which must form a streamlined shape for supersonic flying, has to droop for landing. There are, in fact, four positions of the combined visor and nose. Three of them are used on every flight.

The nose and visor are fully up at all speeds above an indicated airspeed (see page 134) of 250 knots – equal to about 290 mph.

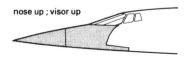

The visor alone can be lowered (it slides down and forward into a recess in the nose), but this position is seldom used, except at a transit stop, when the windscreen needs cleaning.

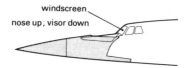

windscreen
nose up, visor down

Below 250 knots the angle of attack is beginning to increase –
to about 7 degrees – and the aircraft is likely to be within the
outer traffic pattern of an airfield. In the USA all aircraft below
10,000 feet altitude are required to fly at 250 knots or less, as
they are then in the area where light aircraft, moving at slower
speeds, can fly largely unrestricted. To provide vision along the
flight path, the nose is lowered to its 5 degrees position, giving a
downward view of about 10 degrees. The nose hinges from a
point just below the pilots' seats. This position is also used for
take-off.

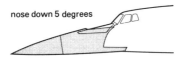

nose down 5 degrees

For landing, once the wheels are down, the nose is lowered all
the way, producing that birdlike appearance which has given
cartoonists so much fun over the years.

nose down 12½ degrees

Oddly enough, the various positions do not much affect the
total drag, but they do affect the noise on the flight deck.
Whenever the visor is down in flight, it becomes hard to hear
normal speech, which is why the crew wear headsets and talk to
each other over the interphone during take-off and approach.
Conversely, raising the visor during the climb-out produces the
most marvellous calm, as if the aeroplane itself has been let off
the bit and has decided to settle down and take things seriously,
now that some real flying is in sight.

The Power Plant

Four Rolls-Royce/SNECMA Olympus 593 Mark 610 engines propel Concorde. Together they produce 152,200 lbs of thrust at take-off and 27,160 lbs of thrust in cruise at 60,000 feet. With their intake and exhaust systems they are among the most technically impressive features of the aeroplane, but they are noisy . . .

Designing a propulsion system for a Mach 2 airliner involves as many compromises as does the design of the wing. The first necessity is that the engines should work successfully in the cruise. This means that they must be narrow in cross-section, to minimize drag, and they must have a high exhaust velocity – for otherwise the exhaust itself would tend to slow the aircraft. Both of these requirements dictate an engine of low by-pass ratio.

All modern subsonic airliners use engines of high by-pass ratio. These have a number of advantages, including their com-

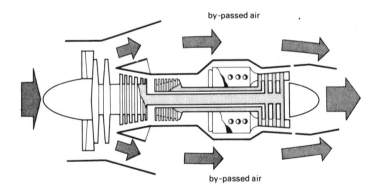

Fan-jet (high by-pass ratio) engine

parative quietness, because their huge fans, acting like propellers, move a large mass of air slowly, whereas a pure jet moves a smaller mass of air faster.

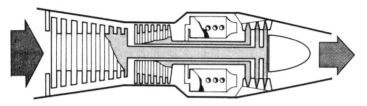

Pure jet (low by-pass ratio) engine

As the major component of aircraft noise comes from the mixing of the exhaust with the static air outside (a 'tearing' effect), the disadvantages of the pure jet are obvious, but there was really no choice. Since the Olympus engine was already in existence and capable of being developed to the power necessary for Concorde, it was selected early on in the programme.

A suitable engine, however, is only the beginning of a supersonic power plant, for no jet engine can accept air in its compressors at supersonic speeds. It is, in fact, necessary to slow it down from Mach 2 to Mach 0·5 before allowing it to enter the engine. This is done over the eleven-foot length of the air intake.

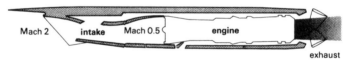

Power plant

The moving parts of the intakes, which are hydraulically powered under computer control, consist of two 'ramps', which move up and down to control the airflow, and two smaller doors, which either let in more air or spill it when it is not required by the engine.

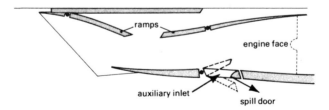

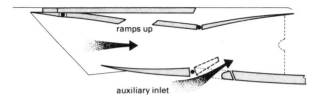

ramps up

auxiliary inlet

At take-off, because the engines need all the air they can get, the ramps are fully up, and the auxiliary inlet is open. By about Mach 0·7, the auxiliary inlet will be closed, and above Mach 1·3 the ramps come into play, lowering to form a series of shock waves starting from the bottom lip of the intake. These have the effect of slowing the air down. By the time Mach 2 has been reached, the ramps have moved over half of their possible

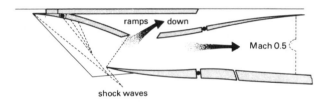

ramps down

Mach 0.5

shock waves

travel. The air is not only slowed down, it is also compressed and considerably raised in temperature. The compression is helpful because it means that the engine's own compressors have less work to do, but the rise in temperature of about 200°C leads to the necessity for special metals in the engine.

As the aeroplane flies along, it meets changes in air temperature and pressure which cause disturbances to the wave pattern in the intakes. The computers sense these changes and make fine adjustments to the positions of the ramps to maintain the airflow needed by the engines. Equally, changes in engine power settings require changes to the airflow. The computers deal with this in the same way.

The most difficult case of change in demand is an engine failure, or shut-down, at high speed. Here, suddenly, the engine requires little or no air. So the ramps go down fully, diverting some of the air over the top of the engine, while the spill door opens wide to pour air out of the underside. The speed of operation of the system is obviously critical. To me, one of Concorde's most impressive features is the intake's ability to deal with anything that comes its way. Slam-closure of a throttle at Mach 2 makes the aeroplane react, but the engine doesn't even hiccup.

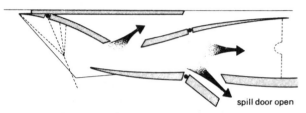

spill door open

This need suddenly to dump air produces the one odd flying characteristic of the aeroplane: if an engine fails at supersonic speed, Concorde banks the wrong way. Any aircraft, Concorde included, will yaw towards a 'dead' engine; thrust on that side has suddenly been lost, and the engine has become a producer of drag. As a result, the wing on the side opposite to the failed engine will temporarily move faster, gain lift and rise.

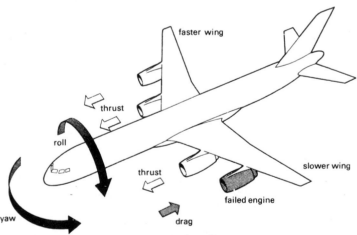

Engine failure – subsonic aircraft

The combined effect is both roll and yaw towards the dead engine.

But at Mach 2 there is all that excess air to get rid of. The spill door opens and the intake air is deflected downwards. This causes the wing to rise and the aircraft to bank away from the

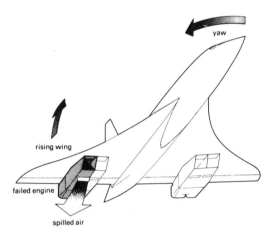

Engine failure – Mach 2

dead engine. The technique for dealing with this situation is first to level the wings, then to counter the yaw with rudder. The autostabilizers will already have applied some rudder so it is not a difficult process, once learned.

Each intake, then, presents high-pressure hot air at Mach 0·5 to the first stage of the Olympus engine, which is itself a conventional two-spool turbojet fitted with an afterburner.

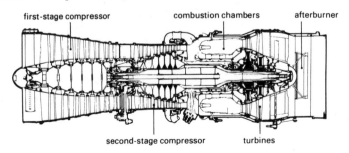

The engine

The power of a jet engine is controlled essentially by the amount of fuel injected into the combustion chambers. The compressors react to changes in fuel flow by speeding up or slowing down to provide the appropriate mass of air to mix with the fuel. The pilots' throttles (or thrust levers) are the principal means of varying power, but here, as with the flying controls, the signalling is electrical, to an Engine Control Unit which sets limits of temperature and rotation rate for various parts of the engine. This means that the crew need not worry about the speed at which they move the throttles – the control unit will make sure that the engines respond at the best possible rate.

Afterburners are simply a method of making use of the hot exhaust gases once they have passed through the turbines. Fuel is sprayed into a ring in the exhaust pipe and burned to increase thrust when it is required: on take-off and during acceleration through Mach 1. These are the two most power-demanding periods of flight. An engine powerful enough to cope with them would be too powerful for the cruise, and probably heavier as well. Concorde's afterburners increase thrust on take-off by about 25 per cent, but they do make heavy demands on fuel, causing nearly a ton of fuel to be burned between the start of a heavy-weight take-off and 1000 feet on the climb.

The last component of the power plant is the variable exhaust. This is an arrangement of hinged 'buckets' or 'clamshells'

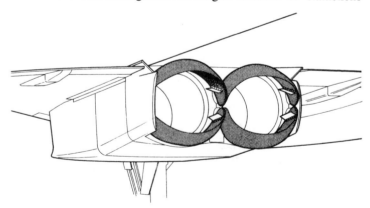

Variable exhaust

whose position can be varied to control the exhaust in the most efficient way. At take-off they close slightly, allowing air to be sucked in from outside for mixing with the exhaust. This reduces noise, as well as improving engine performance.

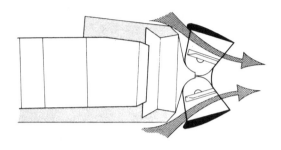

Take-off

During the climb they progressively open until, soon after passing through Mach 1, they are acting as an expansion chamber.

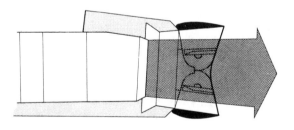

Supersonic

The same system acts as a thrust reverser on all four engines on the ground (to assist braking), and on the two inboard ones in the air (to increase the rate of descent).

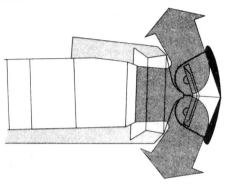

Reverse thrust

The intake and variable exhaust systems are together responsible for a good deal of the aeroplane's thrust development – about half of the thrust at Mach 2 is due to their combined effect.

Navigation

Concorde's navigational equipment is fairly conventional. At the time its substance was decided, the Boeing 747 had just been introduced into service, and major advances had been built into its flight deck and navigation systems. There were obvious savings in making Concorde's arrangements as similar as possible to the 747's. The only real differences in the two aircraft's navigational needs were in the areas of speed and precision. Obviously Concorde moved a great deal faster, and it was already clear that we were going to need to keep it very accurately on track to control the potentially anti-social effects of the sonic boom.

Flight over most of the inhabited parts of the world is conducted on 'airways' – routes in the sky defined by radio beacons. Concorde carries all the equipment needed to follow these routes – at least two of each type in case of failure. Most long-range aircraft carry inertial navigation systems (INS) for overwater flight. Concorde has three of these.

An INS is a combination of very accurate gyros and accelerometers, electronically connected to each other through a small
computer. Once started, it is completely independent of any outside source of information except the force of gravity and the

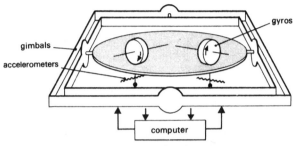

INS – mechanics

accelerations of the vehicle in which it is mounted. At start-up it
need be told only its position in order to allow it to align itself
both horizontally and with True north. This position is also
used as a starting point from which to begin calculations of
position once the aircraft moves. From then on, all accelerations, however small, are integrated by the computer and turned
into changes of position. Using its knowledge of change of

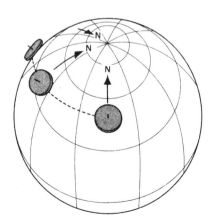

INS – navigating

position, the computer then precesses (twists) the gyros so as to realign the platform with the new horizontal. The whole system works as if it were tied to the centre of the earth and to True north. This effectively produces a grid of latitude and longitude in which position can be described.

An inertial platform (as the measuring part of the assembly is known) is very largely self-correcting, and the systems in use in the airlines produce an average error rate of about one mile per hour of flight. So after a subsonic ocean crossing of, say, four hours, the probable error would be four miles. Inertial navigation is particularly suitable for supersonic flight, as speed does not affect the error, but the shorter flight-time curtails its growth. So, on a similar supersonic flight the probable error would therefore be two miles – good, but not quite good enough for Concorde's particular needs.

To limit the growth of error, the three computers are made to work in committee. In each one, all three positions are compared, and a 'best estimated position' is continuously worked out. This position, which is the one displayed on the instruments and acted upon by the crew, is accurate to better than half a mile per hour – about one mile at landfall.

This portion of the supersonic flight is where accuracy needs to be tightest, as one might be running along the Bristol Channel towards London, or down the eastern seaboard of the USA on the way to New York or Washington. Here navigation aids on the ground help to refine the position. DME (Distance Measuring Equipment) is used. Radar pulses are sent out from the aircraft, and these trigger off replies from a particular ground station, depending on the frequency selected. The time interval between the transmission and reception of the pulses defines the distance between the aircraft and the ground transponder. The computers know the position of the ground station and can calculate its expected distance from the aircraft. Any difference between this and the measured distance is clearly an error. Once a DME is tuned, and the 'updating' process is started, any error begins to be corrected. As the measurements are taken continuously, the computers are allowed to 'wash out' the errors gradually. Generally, by the time one is abeam a DME station up to 200 miles away, the accuracy of position is better than half a mile.

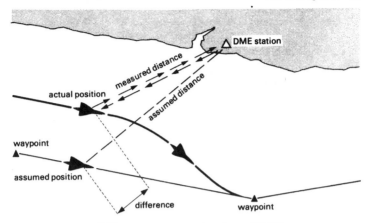

INS – error correction from DME

Knowing accurately where you are at any one time is a great help, but it is also necessary to travel along a precisely defined route. To do this it is necessary to communicate with the computer, through its Control and Display Unit (CDU). The switch

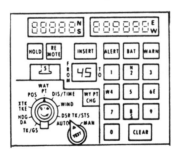

INS – CDU

at the bottom left corner selects what is to be displayed at the top, and a large variety of data is available. Routes are defined by waypoints (WAY PT on the selector). These are simply points, defined by latitude and longitude, over which you want the aircraft to fly. Up to nine such points can be typed in and stored in the computer.

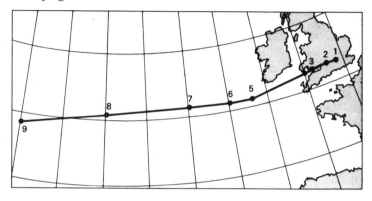

INS – waypoints

When waypoints are passed, they become available for re-programming. As the computer cycles through the list, returning to Waypoint 1 after Waypoint 9, a whole new sequence can begin. To take part of the labour out of reprogramming the waypoints, which on some routes can occur every few minutes, a simple optical card reader is used.

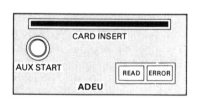

Card reader

Each card carries all the waypoints for a segment of the route, and three or four are usually enough for a whole flight. The DME stations for use in the updating process are inserted in the same way.

The combined effect of these modifications is to bring standard inertial systems up to Concorde's requirements. The automation of inserting data reduces workload, and the tightening-up of accuracy towards the end of each flight gives the necessary precision.

Inertial systems also provide very accurate attitude and direction information. Their gyros are so finely tuned and stable that they make it possible to dispense with a large number of gyros which were fitted to older aircraft. The inertial systems supply information to the attitude indicators and the compasses (both basic flying instruments), to the radar (for stabilization) and to the autopilots.

The Autothrottles and Autopilots

The slender delta wing, which can produce lift at such surprisingly high angles of attack, has a concomitant penalty: high drag at low speeds. In fact, on approach, Concorde is flying on what pilots know as 'the back side of the drag curve'.

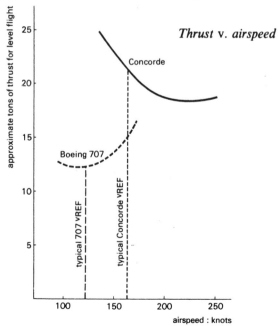

This sounds rather alarming, but one should remember that, first, the wing is still lifting strongly and will continue to do so well below approach speeds, and that there is an enormous reserve of power, as less than half the available thrust is being used. What is true, though, is that any disturbances to the airspeed need quick response from the engines. For this reason, Concorde was designed from the start with automatic throttles. These can be used throughout the flight (except on take-off). When they are not actually in use they can be primed, so that, for example, they come into action when one levels out at a preselected altitude. They are primed during the Mach 2 cruise as well, ready to take off power if a sudden temperature change causes a rise in Mach number above 2·04. Most importantly, they are engaged on all approaches whether flown manually or automatically.

Concorde's autothrottles use longitudinal accelerometers to detect changes in the aeroplane's momentum. This allows them to 'see' changes in airspeed almost before they happen, and, consequently, the movements of the throttles, although fast, are much smaller than one might expect, and the control of speed is satisfyingly tight. This is the first really effective autothrottle system I have flown (there have been plenty of sloppy ones), and as a result of experience with Concorde I am convinced that a high-class autothrottle would be a notable addition to the safety of any aircraft.

The controls for the two autothrottles and autopilots are grouped together above the pilots' instrument panels, so that

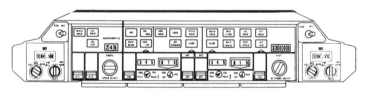

Autopilot and autothrottle panel

both can easily reach them. On the left are the autothrottle controls. The two 'piano keys' engage them, and the buttons are pressed to select the various modes of operation: MACH HOLD and IAS HOLD, which cause the system to maintain a particular Mach number or airspeed, and IAS ACQ (indicated airspeed acquire), which demands the speed set in the selector. Both autothrottles can be engaged at the same time; one will be active while the other follows up, ready to take over if the first fails.

The autopilot controls take up the rest of the panel. The two control switches engage them. Only one can be engaged at a time, except during an automatic landing, when the second can be used for back-up purposes. There are five horizontal and twelve vertical modes.

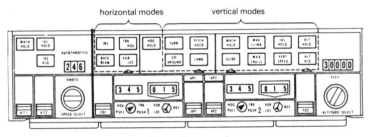

Autopilot panel

The abundance of methods of control in the vertical demonstrates the modern tendency to concentrate on height-keeping for safety reasons. On the far right is the altitude selector. In common with most modern aircraft, this is used throughout the flight, whether or not the autopilot is in use, and warns of arrival at, and departure from, the altitude set in the window.

Some of these seventeen modes will be found on all airliners, and nearly all on some, but the two labelled MAX CLIMB and MAX CRUISE are unique. They are used, in the climb and cruise, to hold the aircraft within three maximum values: indicated airspeed, Mach number and skin temperature. The indicated airspeed can be as high as 530 knots, the maximum Mach number is 2·02 and the highest allowable skin temperature (at the hottest point of the aircraft – the nose probe) is 127°C. The MAX CLIMB mode slows the aeroplane down by pitching it up as any of these values is reached, and the MAX CRUISE mode does the same, except that the rate of pitch control is reduced and instead, if the Mach number is exceeded, it engages the autothrottle in order to reduce the speed. This prevents the aeroplane from 'chasing' sudden changes in Mach number by climbing or diving, as such changes, mostly due to small variations in temperature, are usually temporary. With MAX CRUISE engaged, an increase in Mach number will cause the autothrottle MACH HOLD button to light up, showing that it has come into action; the throttle levers move back a little, the Mach number reduces, the throttles go forward again, and the flight path has stayed undisturbed.

Automatic landings (the LAND mode) are very similar on all the latest generation of airliners. The airport Instrument Landing System (ILS) is used to provide guidance. Two radio transmitters near the runway define paths in space: one horizontal (the localizer) and one vertical (the glideslope) to the

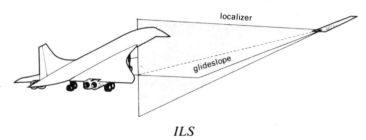

ILS

touchdown point. If the aeroplane is kept on the intersection of both, then it will fly down the centre line and on a 3-degree slope until it arrives on the runway. In fact, just before landing, a radio altimeter, measuring the height between the wheels and the runway, takes over from the glideslope so that the autopilot can flare into a soft touchdown.

Concorde's automatic landings are impressive, because the combination of the high-quality attitude information from the INS, the autostabilization of the flying controls and the precise autothrottles make the holding of the two beams look easy. Although the stick and throttle levers move quite actively the aircraft remains rock steady. Touchdowns are good, too; in fact a little too good for a pilot's ego – one would like to think there is *something* one could do better than the autopilot.

On the other hand, an automatic landing has to be very good to gain pilot confidence – he does not willingly delegate the landing to an autopilot unless it can do it, when he wants it to, better than he can. In fog he cannot see, so he cannot land, but the two autopilots, acting together, with one ready to take over if the other fails, can bring the aeroplane down on ILS to a point of decision over the touchdown area. When Concorde's wheels are fifteen feet above the runway the pilot needs to be able to see ahead a distance of 200 metres (about three runway centreline lights). Provided he can – and he needs this degree of visiblity only to control the roll-out – he will let the aeroplane land itself. If he cannot, he can safely open up the power and go around. The best test of an automatic landing system is pilot opinion: if they like it, it's good, if they don't, it's no good. They like it. They use it whenever the weather demands it, provided the airport is properly equipped. Remarkably enough, only about half of the runways on which Concorde lands are up to standard in this respect.

The autopilot is so comprehensive that one may justifiably wonder what need there is for pilots at all. In fact, autopilots do not in any way replace pilots: they either extend the range of things a pilot can do, or perform time-consuming jobs rather more efficiently. Whether landing in fog, coping with turbulence or following a track, an autopilot has nothing else to do but the task it has been set. A pilot, however, dealing with a complex bit of flying, has little spare capacity for planning, for monitoring or for dealing with emergencies. An autopilot frees him to sit back a little, and to keep a very close eye on what is happening. Over the years the pilot's role has changed: he is less a stick-jockey than he used to be, more in overall control.

The Flight Deck

The first impression is of crowding. It is smaller than most cockpits and there is not quite full headroom. Panels cover most of the walls and roof, and each is closely packed with instruments. It is narrow, because the fuselage is beginning to fine down to the nose. No padded armchairs here, only rather skeletal seats mounted on rails so that they can be powered back and forth.

But install yourself in the left-hand seat (left leg first and head well down, or you may have to be helped out again), and it all begins to fit into place. The instruments are basically familiar to

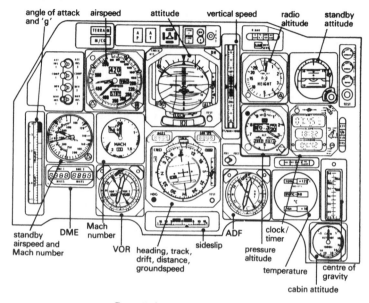

angle of attack and 'g' airspeed attitude vertical speed radio altitude standby attitude

standby airspeed and Mach number DME Mach number VOR heading, track, drift, distance, groundspeed sideslip ADF clock/timer pressure altitude temperature centre of gravity cabin attitude

Captain's instrument panel

any airline pilot, but there are a few new ones, and some of the standard flight instruments display extra pieces of information. For example, the Mach meter has two orange-coloured 'bugs' which enclose the range of Mach numbers available at a current centre of gravity. And at the bottom right of the panel there is

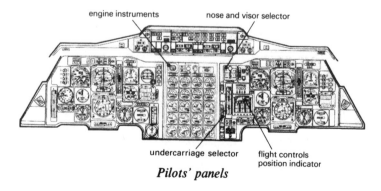

engine instruments nose and visor selector

undercarriage selector flight controls position indicator

Pilots' panels

an indicator on which the centre of gravity is shown, together with the range permissible at the present Mach number.

The pilots' centre panel carries four columns of five engine instruments, and just to the right of them the selectors for the undercarriage and the nose and visor. Further right is an indicator which shows the positions of the elevons and rudders and a duplicate set of flight instruments for the co-pilot.

The centre pedestal contains the INS control and display units, the throttles and afterburner switches, and all the radio controllers. The radar sets are outboard of the two pilots, just behind the nosewheel steering handles.

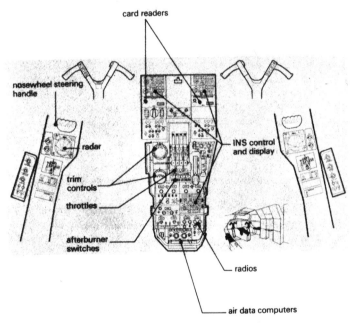

Centre pedestal and side panels

The roof panel carries a number of ancillary switches, including those for lighting, de-icing and probe heating. Here also are the engine high-pressure fuel cocks, flying control selection and changeover switches and the engine fire extinguisher handles.

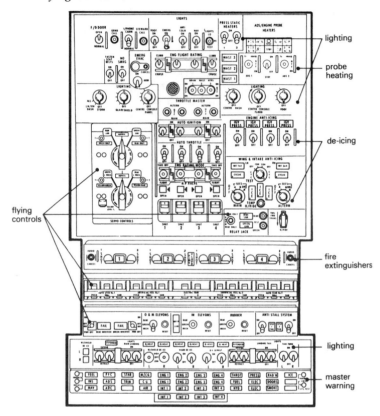

Overhead panel

At the bottom of the roof panel is the Master Warning panel. This is a collection of red and amber captions which light up (with a 'gong' warning) to identify any failed system. With this in front of him, the flight engineer can face forward and motor his seat up to just behind and between the pilots for the take-off and landing.

His own panel is a spectacular-looking affair which, when set up by him, will control automatically the airconditioning and pressurization, fuel and centre of gravity, hydraulics, electrics and oxygen.

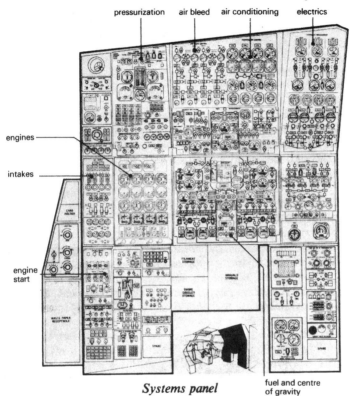

pressurization   air bleed   air conditioning   electrics

engines

intakes

engine
start

Systems panel   fuel and centre
of gravity

It's a complicated little flight deck, but then it's quite a complicated little aircraft. It isn't hard to imagine the design effort which went into all these panels. I remember sitting for hours in a special mock-up trying just to get the lighting right. We shone a high-powered lamp through the windows from every angle to check daylight visibility (bright sunshine can blot out some displays), and sat in the pitch dark to check that every instrument could be seen at night, both by those who like them barely visible (as I do) and by those who like to look out over a panel as brightly lit as a juke box.

After several years of flying in this cockpit, I wish only that the seats were softer, and that there was a little more room to put things, including my left elbow.

3. The Supersonic Environment

The atmosphere in which we live is turbulent. Each day the sun's energy heats the ground which in turn warms the air nearest it. The air expands, takes up water vapour and rises, becoming, through this combination of heat and water, charged with energy of its own.

Temperature

As the air rises it cools and contracts, squeezing out moisture in the form of clouds. In the process of condensation, further cooling takes place. This goes on until no more cooling is possible: the air has run out of energy. Then the reverse happens. The cold air, with nothing left to keep it rising, sinks back towards the

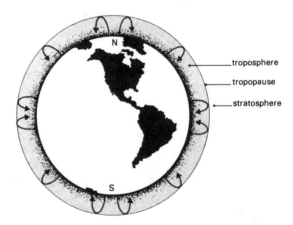

earth, where it disperses to begin the cycle again. The layer in which this heat-triggered circulation takes place is called the troposphere. The point at which most of the circulation stops is called the tropopause. Above the tropopause is the stratosphere, where temperature is relatively stable, and there is no cloud.

The troposphere contains almost all the good and bad weather that go to make up life: on the one hand the continuing cleansing of the air, the re-cycling of moisture, protection from the sun's rays; and on the other hand, floods, frosts and gales. In the stratosphere much less happens – it is clear, peaceful and comparatively inert.

Because at the equator the sun's rays arrive more directly than they do at the poles, the energy imparted to the rising air is

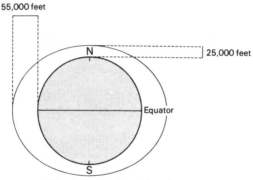

much greater, and it rises further. So, the tropopause can be as high as 55,000 feet at the equator, and as low as 25,000 feet at the poles. Rising air cools at about 2°C per 1000 feet until it

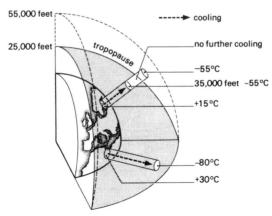

reaches the tropopause, so at a high altitude (say, 55,000 feet) over the equator, the air is considerably colder than at the same height in temperate latitudes. These are not unusual figures – this pattern of temperature seems always to be present at Concorde's cruising altitudes of between 50,000 and 60,000 feet. Because the engines are air-breathing, colder, denser air produces more thrust, and so in tropical regions the aircraft quickly reaches its maximum height of 60,000 feet, whereas on the transAtlantic run it seldom gets above 57,000 feet.

The troposphere, as well as bellying out in the tropics, shifts from season to season, following the influence of the sun.

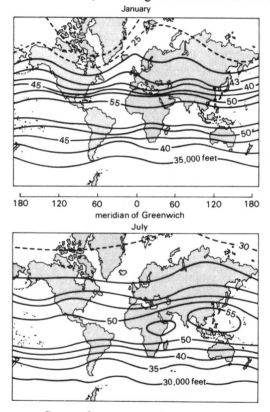

Seasonal movement of the troposphere

It also has its discontinuities and quirks. In high latitudes the air in the stratosphere almost always behaves as it should: that is, the temperature does not vary with height. But near the equator there can be a marked 'inversion' (a rise in temperature with increasing height) just above the tropopause.

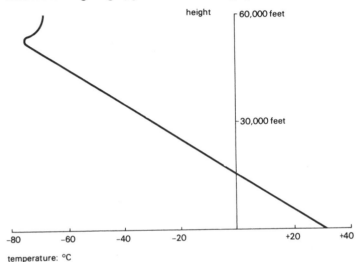

Another feature of the tropical atmosphere is 'temperature turbulence'. This is not turbulence in the sense that the air is disturbed, but rather in that quite small areas of the atmosphere seem to acquire extra energy, perhaps from surface heating, and form discontinuities, or 'bubbles', in the tropopause. In these

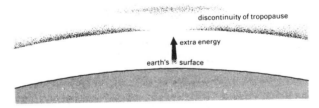

bubbles further cooling will have taken place, and an aircraft flying through them may experience a quite sudden drop in air temperature (perhaps 5°C or so), shortly followed by an equal rise back to normal, as it flies out of the bubble.

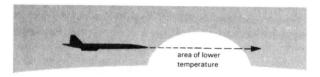

area of lower
temperature

The effect of both these phenomena is the same: a temporary change in Mach number. Since the speed of sound varies with temperature, attempts to maintain a particular Mach number by pitching the aircraft up or down can lead to a rather unsatisfactory hunt around the upper atmosphere, in conditions which are likely to be changeable, and therefore unhelpful. If, on the other hand, the aircraft's flight path is left relatively undisturbed, but small and temporary adjustments are made to the power, passage through these areas is quite simple. The only noticeable effect is that the Mach number may vary between about 2·04 and 1·96 during these disturbances.

This cold, lively air is found in the Tropics. Warm (or comparatively warm) air brings its own problems. Concorde is built principally of aluminium alloys, and it has to be flown at temperatures which will preserve its structural life. At Mach 2, the friction of air passing around the aircraft heats its skin considerably. The maximum heating occurs on the very tip of the nose, which is where it is measured. At this point the rise in temperature is about 175°C over that of the surrounding air. Further back, along the fuselage and wings, the temperature decreases.

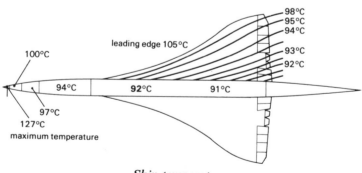

Skin temperatures

Of course, the hotter the air outside, the hotter the skin gets. At a temperature of 127°C on the nose, the crew takes action to lessen the friction by reducing the Mach number – to 1·98 or so. In fact, no speed is lost, since the lower Mach number, at a higher temperature, will produce the same true air speed. The particularly warm upper atmosphere which causes this exists occasionally over the North Atlantic in winter, when the tropopause is at its lowest point.

This heating by friction happens only to aircraft travelling supersonically. The skin of a subsonic aircraft cools down as it climbs into colder air, warming up again as it descends. Concorde's goes through two cycles on each flight, cooling on the early part of the climb, heating rapidly between Mach 1 and Mach 2, cooling again as it slows to subsonic speeds, and finally warming once more as it descends towards its destination.

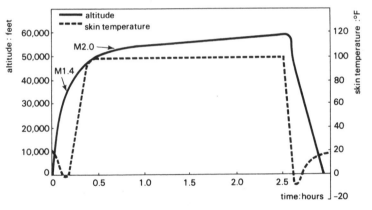

Temperature cycle

These cycles of heating and cooling are accompanied, naturally enough, by expansion and contraction. The fuselage grows several inches in length between take-off and Mach 2; hard to see, but it is possible to watch the rear edge of the flight engineer's panel rejoin the bulkhead behind it during the descent, closing a gap of nearly an inch. There is really nothing surprising about this – all aircraft expand and contract in flight. Concorde does so rather more than others because of the large temperature range it encounters.

Pressurization

An aircraft's pressurization system is needed to pump up the cabin to a reasonable pressure with air taken in from outside, and to heat or cool it to provide a comfortable temperature. It also has to release used air back to the atmosphere. Concorde's pressurization system has a considerable task to perform. The air it uses may be very thin and cold (in the stratosphere) or very dense and hot (on the ground in the Tropics). Happily, there is very high-pressure air available in the engine compressors, and it is from these that air is bled off into a complex arrangement of heat exchangers and refrigeration units, to provide pressurization and airconditioning. The system does its job well, keeping the cabin pressure at the equivalent of 6000 feet in the cruise, and controlling changes smoothly.

Incidentally, the air in all jet airliners' cabins is extremely dry, and as the hours pass this can lead to some discomfort, particularly around the nose and eyes. Practised travellers drink a good deal of non-alcoholic liquids which slows the dehydration process down (alcohol simply speeds it up). Supersonic flight is a real benefit here – shorter flights mean less dehydration and therefore less discomfort.

A pressurization system must cope with emergencies as well. It, or, more accurately, the aircraft, must be able to keep the cabin to a tolerable pressure during the few minutes it takes to descend to thicker air in the unlikely event of a window blowing out. However powerful the compressors, they could not cope with a hole the size of an ordinary aircraft's cabin window, so Concorde's are a good deal smaller than one would otherwise like them to be. A pity, this, because the view is so good, but there is no reasonable alternative.

Winds

The stratosphere is notable for its lack of energy and its stable temperature (compared with lower levels). But there is also much less wind. In the earth's immediate atmosphere the strongest winds are found near the tropopause, in the middle latitudes. In the northern winter, winds of up to 300 miles per hour have been recorded between 30,000 and 40,000 feet. Perhaps the two most common areas for these 'jet streams' are over north-eastern America and Japan. Jet streams are cores of high-speed air, moving usually along and slightly ahead of a frontal system.

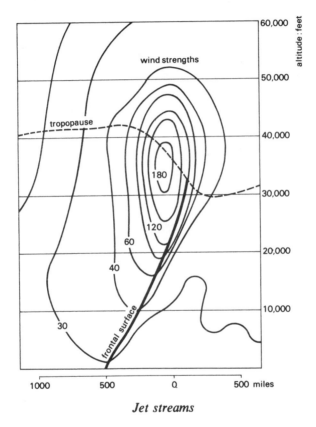

Jet streams

I can remember two journeys in a Comet IV on successive days in January 1961, between Hong Kong and Tokyo, whose flight times were dramatically different as a result of very high winds: from Hong Kong to Tokyo the flight took three hours and forty minutes with the wind behind; the return took six hours and ten minutes.

Generally speaking, winds at Concorde cruising levels are around 50 miles an hour or less, although occasionally in winter they have been measured at 120 miles an hour. Because of these considerably lower wind speeds, and because the aircraft's own speed is so high, eastbound and westbound schedules vary very little – only about fifteen minutes between London or Paris and New York – such difference as there is being mostly due to the subsonic parts of the flight.

Turbulence

Jet streams also produce turbulence. The tunnel of air, moving at a much higher speed than the surrounding air mass, leaves a trail of disturbance around its edges. This is usually the origin of

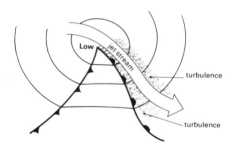

what is known as clear air turbulence (CAT). Flying in it for any length of time is a trying experience which fortunately we largely miss in Concorde.

Each new series of airliners has come with the promise of flying above the weather. None has fulfilled the promise, but there is no doubt that the proportion of each flight spent in turbulent air, associated either with cloud or jet streams, is much lower at SST altitudes. The climb is faster, too, so one usually breaks out of cloud within twenty minutes of take-off, into the smooth stratospheric air. Only in the Tropics does the occasional cumulo-nimbus thunderhead intrude into the calm. There are never any clouds above.

At these heights Concorde cruises at Mach 2. The term 'Mach number' has appeared fairly often already, and it will appear again – perhaps a digression is necessary.

Mach Number

The expression has been used so far as if it were a measure of speed, but this is not quite true. In fact it is a comparison between the aircraft's speed and the speed of sound. Thus Mach 1 is equal to the speed of sound, Mach 2 twice the speed of sound, and so on. Sound travels by transmitting minute pressure waves through the air. The warmer the air, the faster they travel. As temperature falls with increasing altitude, so does the speed of sound: from about 765 mph at sea level to 665 mph in the stratosphere. At the speed of sound, air changes its behaviour, causing the pattern of airflow around an aircraft to change as well. Mach number provides an important datum point, both for the designer and for the crew, expressing speed with reference to the behaviour of the air.

Up to the tropopause, when air temperature is falling, the air speed for any Mach number is reducing. Above the tropopause, which for this purpose is assumed to be 36,500 feet, temperature is constant with increasing height, so Mach number becomes a direct expression of air speed: Mach 1 is 665 mph, Mach 1·5 is 997·5 mph, Mach 2 is 1330 mph. In practice, on any of Concorde's routes which are outside the Tropics, one should be above the tropopause by Mach 1·5 on the climb, so the cabin Machmeter can be used to calculate the air speed quite precisely.

A less accurate, but still quite effective method, is to move the decimal place of the Mach number one digit to the right. This gives a fairly close approximation to the airspeed in nautical miles per minute. To convert nautical to statute miles, add 15 per cent (or multiply by 1·15). An example:

      Mach number = 1·5
      move decimal = 15·0 nautical miles per minute
      + 15 per cent = 17·25 miles per minute
    For mph, × 60 = 1035 mph

This works quite well right through the range of Mach numbers and heights at which Concorde flies. This range, the aerodynamic habitat, is called 'the flight envelope'.

The Flight Envelope

The envelope of a typical subsonic jet is quite similar to Concorde's up to just below Mach 1, although biased a little towards lower speeds. Usually their maximum altitudes are about 41,000 feet (although some ultra long-range versions and a few business jets go higher), and they cruise at around Mach ·82. Concorde's envelope goes up to 60,000 feet and Mach 2·04.

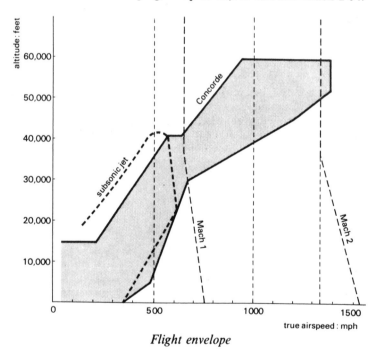

Flight envelope

The normal climb, cruise and descent take place along predetermined paths in the flight envelope, the only usual variation being the height at which the deceleration and descent begin.

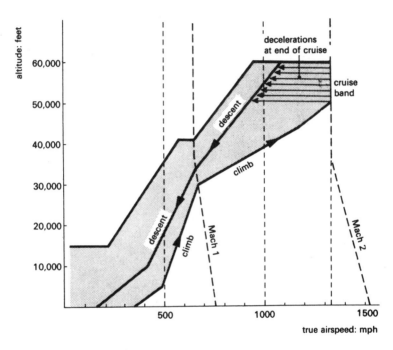

Climb, cruise and descent

Both passenger cabins have a Machmeter mounted on the front wall. Some knowledge of the flight envelope turns them into useful guides to the height of the aircraft, as well as its speed, at any point in a flight.

Part of flight	Mach number	Speed (mph)	Height (feet)
Initial climb	·42	290	Variable – up tc 10,000 in the USA
Subsonic climb	·7	525	9000
	·8	600	17,000
	·9	640	23,000
Subsonic cruise	·95	660	Between 26,000 and 29,000
Acceleration/climb	1·00	675	29,000 on straight climb Can be up to 33,000
	1·2	810	35,000
	1·4	940	38,500
	1·6	1070	42,000
	1·8	1200	45,500
	2·0	1330	50,000 to 60,000
Deceleration	2·0 to 1·65	Slowing to 1100	Level at last cruise height
Descent	1·4	950	52,500
	1·2	810	44,500
	1·0	665	Between 35,000 and 39,000
Subsonic cruise	·95	650	Between 35,000 and 39,000
Descent	·8	570	23,000
In the circuit	·42	290	Below 10,000 in the USA or approaching the airfield
	·32	220	Turning on to final approach
	·26 to ·28	180–190	Final approach

Concorde begins to be really effective when it travels well above Mach 1. But at these higher Mach numbers certain other effects begin.

The Boom

Sonic booms are caused by shock waves. Any object moving through the air – a powered aircraft, a bird, even a glider – causes disturbances which travel outwards, like ripples. These ripples move at the speed of sound, because that is what they are – sound waves – although in many cases they are far too feeble to be heard. The air particles ahead of the object receive advance warning of its arrival from these changes of pressure and start to move out of the way. If, however, the object is moving faster than the speed of sound, it arrives before the warning and the air molecules, unable to react in time, build up in front of it. This compression produces a shock wave in the form of a cone.

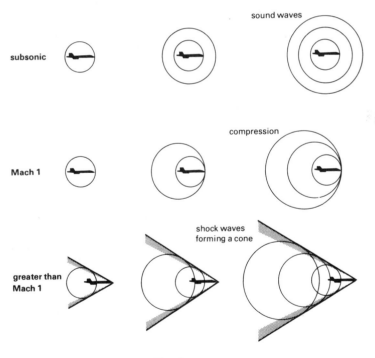

Shock waves

This 'Mach cone' trails behind rather like the bow-wave of a ship moving at speed, except that it is three-dimensional.

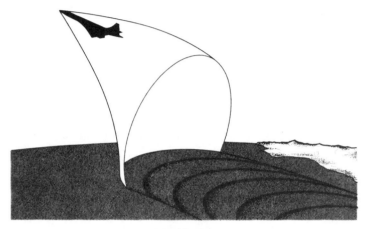

Mach cone

In the same manner as a ship's bow-wave, it is present whenever the aircraft is travelling fast, and its strength decays as it travels outward. Wherever a section of the Mach cone reaches the ground, a boom is heard, some time after the aircraft itself has passed. It lasts only for part of a second, and the pressure change is small, but, because the change in pressure is very sudden, the sound can be startling.

Each type of aircraft produces different patterns of pressure change at supersonic speeds. The shock waves around its structure tend to coalesce into two: one on the nose and one at the tail. A small fighter will produce a double boom whose peaks and troughs of pressure are so close together as to be almost indistinguishable from each other – Concorde's 'signature' is a quite distinct double boom.

The factors which make a boom relatively loud or quiet when it reaches the ground are the weight and height of the aircraft, and the atmospheric conditions. The boom generated by Concorde at Mach 2 above 50,000 feet increases the air pressure on the ground by about 0·1 per cent during its passage. This level of pressure is felt directly underneath. To each side of this the 'over-pressure' reduces until at a distance of about twenty-five miles from the track it is usually detectable only as a dull rumble.

During the acceleration, when the aircraft is both climbing and speeding up, a 'focused' boom reaches the ground. This focusing is the arrival of a series of booms at the same place, each travelling at the same speed but from an accelerating aircraft.

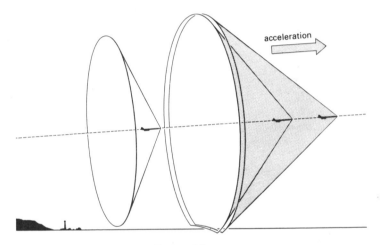

Focused boom

Unlike the main 'boom carpet', which follows the aircraft through supersonic flight, this is confined to a narrow, crescent-shaped area, only about one hundred yards in depth, across part of the track. In this area the intensity of the boom is at its greatest.

There is one further feature of the boom which is of interest, because it was unknown until reports of booms heard over western England and France began to filter in during the winter of 1976/7. The times of observation agreed roughly with Concorde's crossing times on the return journey from the USA, and although they were of much lower intensity than any normal cruise booms, the fact that they appeared at regular times made them noticeable.

The data were studied at Bristol University and an explanation slowly emerged. At the time there was a region of exceptionally high cosmic wind (at about 150,000 feet) over the western Atlantic, and this caused the upward-travelling part of the Mach cone (which normally dissipates in space) to be refracted downward again.

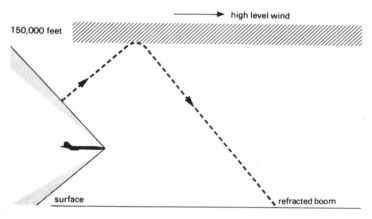

Refracted boom

As knowledge of this phenomenon grew, the public's concern dwindled. Perhaps there was a suspicion that the crews had become cavalier in their attitude to boom control, but they most certainly had not. It is now possible with some degree of accuracy to predict the phenomenon and to take preventive action.

Some odd bits of information came out of the studies. Pheasants, whose ears are particularly sensitive to very low-frequency sounds, were able to hear the reflected booms seconds before humans, and flew away. People indoors sometimes heard a much louder sound than others outside; they were always in rooms with at least one large picture-window, which acted as an amplifier for the rumble outside and turned it back into a boom through the vibration of the glass.

Before Concorde went into service, the boom was one of the central arguments against supersonic flight. The builders had assumed that flight above Mach 1 would be permitted overland.

After all, military aircraft had done so for years over many countries, and no great alarm had been caused. But Concorde would obviously be much bigger than any military aircraft, and there might be many more flights by civil airliners than there had been by the military. The public had a right to be worried.

Tests of the effect of booms on the public were carried out in the USA between 1961 and 1967. The largest and most thorough test took place over several months at Oklahoma City in 1964. Other areas included in the series were St Louis, Chicago, Milwaukee, Pittsburgh and Edwards Air Force Base, California. In Britain, in 1967, eleven flights were made over Bristol and London. As a result of all these, and of later Concorde tests it became clear that supersonic flight over populated areas was not likely to be acceptable, and in due course the USA, Canada, France and Britain produced legislation to ban it.

The airlines had assumed for several years that this would be the case, and looked for routes which were principally over the sea, or over areas of very low population density. Such routes as became available were planned with great care, and crews were trained thoroughly in the characteristics of the boom and methods of ensuring that it did not reach banned areas.

I believe the effort has been successful. There have been very few complaints since regular services began, and those have mostly concerned the mild reflected boom described earlier. There was one well-authenticated boom on the east coast of the USA which, because it coincided with a Concorde arrival, led to a flurry of excitement. It turned out to have been caused by some military aircraft having a little illicit fun flying formation with our aircraft, unknown to us.

Radiation

The atmosphere surrounding the earth protects it from the constant streams of radiation from outside the solar system. Some radiation, however, gets through: more at the poles than the equator. This galactic energy produces the background to the doses of radiation we receive from other sources such as radiography, television sets and the debris of nuclear weapon tests. As an aircraft climbs, it progressively loses some of the protection afforded by the atmosphere. Concorde, at cruise altitudes, receives about twice the dose-rate of a subsonic aircraft. However, because it flies more than twice as fast, the result for any flight distance is the same. Considerably higher doses are received on long, near-polar flights by subsonic aircraft.

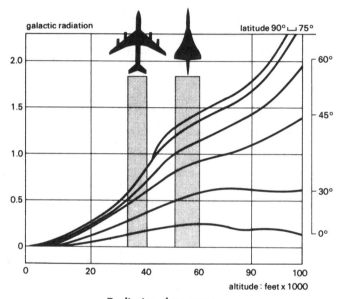

Radiation dose rates

The atmosphere also receives occasional bursts of radiation from the sun. This type of radiation is caused by solar flares. It is of much lower energy than the galactic variety, and so becomes absorbed by the atmosphere. At altitudes above 50,000 feet, the atmospheric protection is small, so the dose-rate can be high. Fortunately these events are rare, as sun spot activity seems to occur on a roughly twelve-year cycle, with peaks every 180 years or so. The next forty years are expected to be on one of the lower curves of the cycle of activity.

Fortunately, also, solar radiation can be forecast, as it reaches our atmosphere about a day after the activity is seen on the sun. It can also be measured on the aircraft by a radiation meter.

Developed by the United Kingdom Atomic Energy Authority, the meter shows dose-rates in the standard units of milliREM per hour. It produces warnings at 10 mREM/hour (Alert), and 50 mREM/hour (Action), and is connected to the Master Warning System in front of the pilots.

It should always be clear, from the daily forecasts, if there is any likelihood of solar radiation, but, in any event, protection from an unpredicted burst of radiation is simple: the aircraft must be returned to the thicker air. So a descent is carried out to an altitude below 47,000 feet and the flight continued at a safe dosage level.

Radiation meter

Even after such a descent the meter is an advantage, as one can tell exactly how effective the action has been, and descend further if necessary. In normal flight the meter needle wavers between ·5 and 1 milliREM/hour. The only occasions on which I have ever seen it go into the 'Alert' segment were when flying over a military installation in a country which, for reasons of tact, I shall not name. As it happened several times, and always in the same place, presumably the radiation was reaching us from below.

Concorde's Effect on the Stratosphere

In January 1975, the report of the Climatic Impact Assessment Programme (CIAP) was published. Sponsored by the US Department of Transportation, it finally laid to rest most of the wilder theories about the effect of SSTs on the atmosphere; at least, it did for those minds not totally committed to the belief that everything about SSTs was bad. The two principal theories were, first, that the water vapour and carbon dioxide emitted from the aircraft's exhausts would cause climatic changes; second, that nitrous oxides (NOx) emitted from the same source would react with the ozone found in the stratosphere and thus reduce the earth's protection from ultra-violet light. The predicted climatic changes included the melting of the polar ice caps, and the supposed reduction of ozone would lead to an increase in non-melanomic (benign) skin cancer.

The CIAP report, based on a vast study, showed that the current fleet of subsonic jets have considerably greater potential effect on the atmosphere than all the SSTs now flying, or likely to, and that even that effect, although calculable, is too small to measure. Observations made between 1961 and 1970 from seven stations around the world showed a slight increase in ozone – during a period when large numbers of subsonic jets were flying, often in the stratosphere. In fact it seems that the cleansing effect of air circulation does extend far up into the stratosphere, and its ability to cope with vastly powerful natural occurrences such as volcanic eruptions should give us confidence.

Airport Noise

Not negligible, however, is the noise of four Olympus 593 engines at full throttle with afterburners, thrusting 180 tons of aeroplane upwards from a runway.

There is not, although many people would like to believe there is, any direct method of comparing the noisiness of different aeroplanes. One can compare the length of two objects easily enough: the concept of length is well understood by everyone, and there are common units of measurement. The word 'noise', however, means different things to different people, and the same noise can arouse opposite emotions in two people with separate tastes. Noise is measured in units based on the decibel (dB). Any noise is a combination of sound waves on different frequencies, so a measure of noise must make some assumptions about which frequencies are most important. dB(A) and dB(D) are two commonly used measurements which produce averages weighted towards lower and higher frequencies. Then there are measurements of Perceived Noise (PNdB) which look at a group of frequencies which have been judged by experiment to be the most important to the human ear. Equivalent Perceived Noise in Decibels (EPNdB) takes into account the duration of the noise as well.

This is not an exhaustive list, although it is complicated enough. I provide it simply to show that comparisons based on them can quickly become confusing unless conducted by experts who have started by laying down ground rules for any discussion. Even then, comparing aircraft involves taking into account their weight, their position and the weather conditions.

Common sense, however, and simply listening, can tell us that Concorde's straight-jet engines are noisier than more modern fans, and that the predominant sound is low-frequency. The challenge presented to us was to make Concorde acceptable to the communities over which it would be flying, and the way to do this was through intense study of its particular noise characteristics. This led to the design of flying techniques which were extraordinarily effective at minimizing community noise. Experience in service showed early on that we could accurately devise the best procedure for any runway, and that the pilots could fly these patterns with great accuracy and repeatability.

But the acid test would always be the reaction of the people living around the airports, once services had settled down into a regular pattern. This test we have passed – Concorde is certainly tolerable to the communities it serves, perhaps more so than some other aircraft.

4. Adapting

BOAC had been involved in studies of potential SSTs since 1954, when the British government formed a group for that purpose. Along with Pan American and Air France, it had taken out sales options for Concorde in 1963, and consequently the three airlines formed the first customer committee – known as the Troika. This committee, like those formed for other aircraft, such as the Boeing 747, came into being because the airlines and the aircraft manufacturers were determined to see that the coming advances in technology, size and speed were handled in a controlled way. They were eager to standardize flight decks and equipment, so that pilots could transfer easily from one aircraft to another, and so that aeroplanes could be sold from one airline to another without major difficulties in crew training. They wanted to be able to borrow each other's spare parts. They reasoned that it wasn't really necessary for airliners to be tailor-made for individual buyers. These committees discussed all new types with their manufacturers, and brought a concerted airline view to bear on each design as it grew.

When I started development work, the Troika meetings, held alternately in Bristol and Toulouse, were already in full swing. The first one I attended was at Bristol. The atmosphere was fascinating. On one side of an enormous table were assembled representatives of the British Aircraft Corporation (BAC) and Aerospatiale, the airframe builders; and of Rolls-Royce and SNECMA, responsible for the engines. On the other side were ranged pilots and engineers from the three airlines. Specialists came and went as their systems were reviewed. Each leader of a design team would present an up-to-the-minute survey of his area of responsibility, at the end of which he would be questioned in detail. If he had a weight addition or an increase in complexity to announce, he would tread nervously to the podium, waiting for the storm.

My boss, Captain Jimmy Andrew, was an engineer-turned-pilot who possessed a very clear view of what the airlines needed from any aeroplane. He also had a remarkably sharp brain and an acerbic wit. It was not wise to present him with a scheme that showed even a trace of woolliness. Many design engineers returned to their offices smarting from his dissection of their proposals, but they came back with better answers. Captain Scott Flower, the doyen of development pilots, represented Pan American. He was nearing the end of his long career, which stretched back to the acceptance work on Pan American's first flying boats. He had dealt with more manufacturers than this one had built planes. To him an SST was just another aircraft, even if it was kind of fast.

Some of the manufacturer's schemes seemed, in airline terms, wildly unrealistic. Scott Flower could be relied upon to react to them with a flourish. Small, grizzled and crew-cut, he wore gold-rimmed reading glasses. At suitable moments his head would appear from behind a pile of documents and, looking over his glasses, he would deliver a stream of down-home reminders of what this whole thing was about – airline flying. Never mind the politicians, forget the delicacy of the relationship between the French and the British – if anybody wanted to *sell* this machine, this *thing*, it had better be the way the airlines wanted it. Occasionally, when apparently too far tried, he would walk out. All this might have been harder to take if he had not usually been right. This over-complicated project regularly needed to be brought to earth.

Meetings in Toulouse were more formal, partly because both the French and English languages were used, with a simultaneous translation service which brought its own (often welcome) touches of anarchy to the proceedings. A bend in the flying control runs was referred to, in English, as a 'dog-leg'. In the hands of a replacement translator, faithful to the language but baffled by the technicalities, this became '*jambe de chien*'. Occasionally a speaker, meaning to be helpful, would slip across the two languages. A Frenchman, for example, might insert an English phrase into his explanation, only to have it promptly put back into French by the equally helpful translator. Into lulls would break the sounds of test transmissions, mysteriously picked up by the headphones from the radios of 001, being assembled in the hangar below.

Light relief of this sort was needed, because real tensions lay behind much of the heat generated inside the conference rooms (heat which, incidentally, rarely lasted outside them). The aircraft had already been a long time in gestation, and the differences in the French and British design approaches had survived long after the inter-governmental agreement of 1962 which had combined their SST schemes into one. Some of the design engineers had worked on no project but Concorde. Much of their experience was with military aircraft. These factors, not lack of talent (no aircraft design can have been blessed with so much of that) contributed to their occasional lack of realism.

On the other side of the table, the design team had good cause to be suspicious of some of the airlines, whose intentions were not always clear. BAC, in particular, was aggrieved at BOAC's cancellation of part of its VC10 order – relations between the airline and the British aircraft industry had been stormy for some years. Pan American, like BOAC, were known to be interested in the US SST, and their Concorde option may have been intended chiefly to spur the US government into getting that project under way. The atmosphere between the Anglo-Saxons was arms-length and edgy.

Between the various French parties, no such difficulties seemed to exist. French aviation affairs appeared to be unified, centrally directed. Such arguments as they had took place privately. Air France's representatives performed a useful but comparatively peaceful role.

This kind of work, in the customer committee, which was directed towards making the aircraft fit in with airline practices, was, of course, only part of the story – the airlines were also taking a hard look at their own methods, to see how they needed to be adapted to supersonic travel. When, in July 1972, BOAC and Air France signed contracts to buy Concorde, a new urgency was given to the preparations. Promised delivery in 1975 meant that our airline needed to start defining in detail just how the aircraft would be flown, by its own crews.

Airline flying differs from other kinds of aviation because its objectives are different. Test flying, for example, is, as its name implies, principally about discovery. Test crews deliberately explore areas outside the flight envelope which the airline pilot, just as deliberately, avoids. They induce engine surges, pull high 'g' forces, go too fast, too slowly – in short, they look for trouble. Their approach to a flight is deliberate and specific; each flight has a purpose different from the one before, and needs to be studied in detail. On the other hand, test crews don't have to worry a great deal about navigation, or about other aircraft, for they are under specialized radar control. They probably return to their own airfield. They minimize the risk by thorough study of the particular day's problems, and, being perhaps the most highly skilled of all pilots, they depend on that skill to get them out of unforeseen difficulties. It remains a risky business, for their main objective is to seek facts about aircraft which are relatively unknown. There is room in test flying for a good deal of individuality. Techniques must to some extent be made up as they go along.

A military pilot's principal objective is to reach his target and destroy it, or, in a different role, to defend it against an attacker. Coming back from a mission is an important, but secondary, objective. He accepts very high risks in war, and even in peacetime he must be bold where a civilian would be cautious.

Success can be measured: in the case of the test pilot, by the degree of exploration he has achieved, and, in the case of the military pilot, by the accuracy of, say, his bombing. An airline pilot can only be said to be successful when he retires. If he does (and I am glad to say that almost all of us do) he will, during his career, have delivered to their destinations something like a million people. His dominant objective will have been safety.

Civil aviation has grown up in the years since the end of the Second World War. Converted bombers gave way to flying boats, which were in turn succeeded by long-range airliners powered by complex piston engines. Then the jet engine arrived, in the form of turbo-props and pure jets. Jet airliners quickly swept away the older types because of the greater efficiency and reliability of their engines. These improvements led to an enormous expansion in the market for air travel because, in real money terms, fares became steadily cheaper. In 1947 only a privileged few, mainly businessmen and officials, flew. Now, happily, it is within almost every young person's range of opportunities to set off around the world carrying nothing more than a backpack. The aircraft in which this revolution has taken place have become larger, faster, internally quieter and freer from vibration. They are also a great deal safer. When I started airline flying in 1957, we used to joke that every take-off was an emergency – a statement which was uncomfortably near the truth. The two aircraft we used to fly on the African routes in those days, Argonauts and Stratocruisers, found taking off from hot, high airfields something of a struggle. The four compound piston engines at full power would reach their maximum cylinder-head temperatures shortly after becoming airborne, and the crew were presented with an unpleasant choice: leave the engine cowl gills open to cool the engines – in which case the drag of the cowls would prevent the speed increasing – or speed up with the gills closed and overheat the engines. Power margins were much lower. Few of the aircraft of the early 1950s would meet today's performance standards, which are based on the ability to climb away safely after an engine failure at the most critical point on take-off.

Jet engines are more reliable than piston engines because they are mechanically much simpler. The four stages of the internal combustion engine cycle – induction, compression, combustion and exhaust – take place in different areas of the jet engine, and

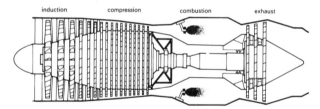

all the parts rotate. In a piston engine they all happen in the same place (the cylinder) and many parts move backwards and forwards.

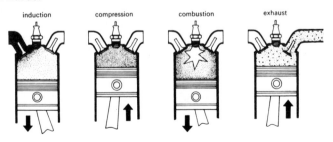

A fairly normal 'time-between-removals' of a compound piston engine was 1200 hours; 6000 hours is a common figure for jets. This enormous improvement in engine reliability has made flying much safer: 'ditching' in mid-ocean, for example, has not happened for many years. But the changes have not only been to the engines and structures – the methods of flying, and even the atmosphere on the flight deck, have changed, too.

A Stratocruiser, carrying about 80 passengers, needed a crew of at least 5: captain, first officer, flight engineer, radio officer and navigator. On some long flights this number could be increased by a relief pilot and flight engineer. The captain tended to be a somewhat isolated figure, in the marine tradition. He did not share his thoughts much with his four assistants whom he expected to perform their specialist tasks in such a way as to provide him with working engines and systems, radio messages and navigational information. This compartmented method of operation was reflected in the design of the cockpit. It was very large, with bulkheads separating some of the crew stations from the others. Heads and arms would appear round them from time to time, passing bits of paper with messages written on them.

Those who filled the different specializations were recognizably different types of people. Flight engineers spent a good deal of time during transit stops on the wings, re-fuelling, or in among the oily engines, looking for defective spark plugs. Their briefcases were full of tools. Navigators tended to be the intellectuals of the profession, and often the entertainers as well – their number included some fine bar-room piano players.

Most of the captains were ex-bomber pilots, and many had developed their own theories about how to avoid storm centres (with no radar), or how to find the most favourable winds. The airspace was much emptier in those days, and an aeroplane could wander at will across deserts or oceans. One captain had a theory about penetrating tropical-line squalls: he would enter them at an angle of 45 degrees and head for the blackest bits. (I hate to think what the picture would have looked like on a radar set.) If it was too rough, he would turn round, come out of the cloud and try again a little further along. He once travelled eastward across a substantial part of West Africa on this saw-tooth pattern before finding a gap and turning north for Rome, which he reached almost two hours late.

Technological advance and pressure to keep down costs eliminated the jobs of the radio officer and navigator. So the crew was reduced to three, while aircraft speed more than doubled. Clearly the remaining crewmen – captain, first officer and flight engineer – needed to be used more efficiently. This has been achieved partly by a steady growth in automation; but just as important has been the change in human terms: the three crew members have become generalists, acting as a closely knit team.

This change in approach to the business of flying occurred gradually at first. The early jets – the Comet, the 707, the DC8 and the Convair 880 – all carried navigators, and the crewmen tended still to behave as specialists. Many airlines found, however, that the systems panels were simple and well-organized enough to be operated by pilots, and the advantages of having a third pilot monitoring the two in the front seats soon became obvious: he was well placed to pick up errors.

The word 'monitoring' has dominated flying procedures ever since. When the Boeing 747, the first of the Jumbos, was ordered by most of the world's major international airlines, a concerted effort was made to re-think cockpit design and complete the process of reducing the crew to three. Many past accidents could by then be traced to two sources: instrument and system designs which induced human error, and unmonitored actions by individual members of the crew. The cure for both of these problems depended on the assumption that humans, although almost infinitely adaptable, could and would make mistakes. It followed, therefore, that all three should monitor each other. Obviously there had to be a commander who took final responsibility, but the three would act in concert, checking each other's work, constantly in communication with one another, understanding each other's jobs.

We took these principles on board Concorde. During the long development period, stretching back to 1960, the flight decks of the prototype and pre-production models had remained specialized: now the flight engineer had to be brought into the operation. (Both British Airways and Air France employ specialist engineers, but they are trained in flying techniques as well, so that they can monitor the pilots.) His seat was powered, so that he could move forward to join the pilots for take-off and landing, and a full set of engine instruments was put on the front centre panel, replacing a large moving-map display which, although a pleasant addition, was not essential. His own area, the systems panel, was designed so that it could be set up to take initial action in the event of any failure, and a master warning panel was added above the windshield to announce failures to all the crew.

The main flying instruments were enlarged, so that they could be read more easily, and the autopilot controls were moved to the top centre of the instrument panel, where, again, all three crew could see what selections had been made. Stowages were arranged for documents and manuals. The instrument lighting was refined.

All these and many more changes produced a flight deck which is similar in appearance and layout to all of Concorde's contemporaries, except that it is much more crowded: there is less panel space, and there are more instruments. The flight deck, then, would seem familiar to new crews – no bad thing when so much else would be unfamiliar.

The procedures by which the aeroplane would be flown needed to be recognizable, too. When converting to a new type of aircraft, an airline pilot takes his past experience with him, like a tool-kit, so it is sensible to base all new methods on practices which have proved successful over the years. Devising new techniques, however, requires a thorough understanding of the special qualities of the aircraft, and a system for getting the best out of each member of the crew.

In the subsonic régime, Concorde behaves very much like other aircraft – speeds are only a little faster – and generally it can be flown in much the same way. There are no flaps and slats, of course, but that is an advantage because it simplifies techniques. Concorde's special features are its speed in the cruise, its more complicated flight envelope, its relative inefficiency at slow speeds, and its potentially anti-social behaviour in terms of sonic boom and airport noise. With these characteristics in mind, it became clear that the crews' work would need to be very well organized.

There are several classic ways of doing this: unnecessary duties can be cut out, checks can be moved away as far as possible from peak periods of workload, and the remaining tasks shared out equally between the three crew members. This kind of rationalization is harder to achieve than it may sound. Every party – the certification authority, the manufacturer, the airline management – has reasons for wanting to add items to the checklists. Although all agree that the lists should be kept short, each tends to resist the removal of any one. But it can be done.

Another method of reducing workload, particularly in supersonic flight, is to do as much of it as possible on the ground – to pre-calculate the answers to questions that are likely to be asked during any flight, to bring forward often-used information from manuals, and to present all this in accessible form for the crew to use. A good example of this approach is the special in-flight navigation chart developed for Concorde. Stripped of inessentials, it shows all the routes, acceleration and deceleration points, coastlines, 'alternate' airfields (with the fuel required to reach them from various points), radio navigation aids, prohibited areas and weather broadcasts. On one piece of paper, which can be folded to fit the standard clip-board, there is a general chart, covering the whole area on a small scale, and more detailed charts for each end of the flight.

Solving operational problems demands a different emphasis for each part of the flight. In the cruise the most important requirement for the crew is to organize themselves so as to cope with the speed – to keep ahead of events. On take-off, and to a lesser extent on landing, we needed to develop special flying techniques. For example, in order to minimize the nuisance of noise for the people living near the airfields we would be using, we analysed the specific problems of noise abatement and looked for solutions. We knew that aircraft noise could be reduced by:

Climbing as steeply as possible after take-off, then throttling to the minimum power to give a safe angle of climb over the communities ... Concorde has a steeper initial climb angle than any other civil aircraft. We could use this with advantage, so as to be higher at the point of power cut-back.

Flying the aircraft, particularly just after take-off, so as to pass over the minimum number of people ... The unusually good stability of Concorde, coupled with the precision of the instruments and controls, makes it possible to manoeuvre more in the early stages of climb, with equal safety.

Keeping the speed as high as possible so as to minimize the duration of the noise . . . Concorde's natural speed after take-off is high – the benefit was there to be taken.

Using the least disturbing runway. There is sometimes a choice available. Knowing which runway will produce least disturbance helps . . . Very comprehensive information was produced on each runway used by Concorde. The captain is able to choose the best runway available on any day.

Keeping the aircraft's weight down. This usually means taking no unnecessary fuel . . . There are many occasions on which excess fuel (which permits more 'holding' time before landing at the destination) can be carried, but fuel costs make this an undesirable luxury for any aircraft. The noise penalty of extra weight was determined. It is a useful factor to take into consideration when deciding the fuel load. This is not, of course, treated as a total bar: it is sometimes prudent to have extra fuel, and when it is, we do.

Choosing schedules at suitable times of the day . . . Concorde's schedules seem naturally to occur at the right times. The predominantly business travellers prefer to take advantage of the short flight-times by making their journeys in daylight. Take-offs are usually between 9 am and 6 pm.

Using noise abatement procedures at all times, even if weight and temperature are low, so as to keep down the average noise over the whole year . . . The average noise is in some ways as important as the peak noise on any particular take-off. An aircraft which just 'beats the monitors' on every take-off may produce an impressive-looking record, but is not being as good a neighbour as it could.

Taking into account all these factors, it was clear that we could develop improved procedures. We were able to produce a basic anti-noise technique which could be varied to suit particular runways at any combination of weight, wind and temperature. The technique could be easily taught and flown. It was thoroughly tested in the simulator and in practice flights in the aircraft. The most stringent failure cases were examined. It only remained to train the crews.

5. Training the Crew

Every captain, co-pilot or flight engineer looks forward to an aircraft conversion course with a mixture of excitement and dread. However much he may enjoy flying his current aeroplane, he is bound to want to try the new equipment: it will contain the latest technology, it will probably be bigger and faster, and its existence is a challenge to his professional pride. On the other hand, he will have to pass the training course, and that means the real possibility of failure, the very idea of which is appalling. Conversion courses generally continue throughout an aircraft's life, and as experience is built up, the training methods improve: members of the early courses are, in effect, guinea pigs. The cost of training is so high that unlimited time cannot be made available for those who fall behind, and so at any point in the course, after due warning, one can be judged unfit to go on.

Aircrew in most airlines select themselves. Their Associations jealously guard their members' right to bid for conversion to any new aircraft. Of the applicants, the most senior win. The course itself, therefore, acts as the filter – those who do not pass return to their previous type. This system, although humanely administered, is harsh – but, then, behind all judgments is the thought that safety is the primary concern, and that anyone who cannot prove his abilities on a conversion course should not be allowed to make the transition to a new aircraft.

It takes about five months to train a Concorde crewman, who will already be experienced on jet aircraft. The first four weeks are spent in a classroom. All aircrew courses nowadays use the 'need to know' principle to confine the content to a reasonable length – it would take years to learn every fact about a complex modern aircraft. Every action required to fly the machine in normal, abnormal and emergency conditions is analysed with the help of a computer and used to define just what it is necessary to learn. Quite elaborate audio-visual aids are used: in France, self-teaching computer terminals perform most of the classroom work, whereas in England electronic working models of the systems are favoured. Both methods seem to take about the same amount of time and to be equally effective.

Ground School

The classroom part of the course, which lasts four weeks – with an extra week beforehand for the flight engineers – is provided by the manufacturers. Even though its content is severely practical, there is a great deal to learn. Aircrew are expected to understand the workings of every system on the aircraft. Many of the systems are familiar, being variations of the existing ones on previous types, but, in Concorde's case, there are some new ones – like the intake controls, which make it possible to fly at Mach 2.

As the course progresses, increasing time is spent in a mockup of the flight deck so that procedures can be practised and familiarity with the instruments and controls built up. At the end of it all comes a very thorough examination, set by the national airworthiness authorities.

The Simulator

There are two Concorde flight simulators: one at Toulouse in the south of France and one at Filton near Bristol. Each is a remarkable machine in its own right. Housed in a large, airconditioned room, it consists of a box mounted on huge hydraulic rams. The box looks from the outside like a truncated front section of an aeroplane. Climb up a ladder on to a platform, step over a retractable bridge into the box, and you are on a flight deck which looks, sounds and almost smells like the real thing. Through the windshield you can see an airport. The seats are powered like the real ones, the instruments are correct. Even the ashtrays are the same as the aircraft's. Lock the door, settle in and go through the checks – everything behaves just as it would on the aircraft. Start the engines and the whine is there, building up slowly – even slight vibrations as the compressors build up speed. Begin to taxi and there is the characteristic nose-wheel bounce.

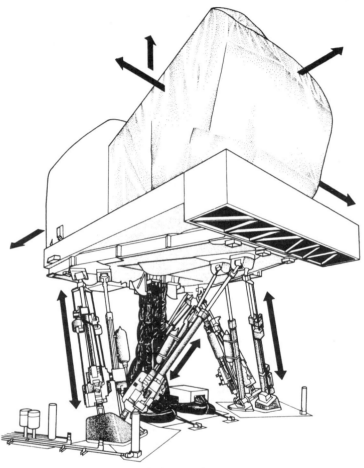

Flight simulator

Despite the existence of a small console into which the instructor can set variables such as the weather conditions, and problems for the crew to cope with, the illusion is very quickly complete. One is flying an aircraft: a Concorde, not a simulator. The response to control movement is extraordinarily accurate, the instruments behave properly even in the most subtle respects, and the noises add an extra bit of conviction.

Another of the features that help to make simulators seem real is the motion system. Controlled, like the rest of the machine, by a computer, the great hydraulic rams can move the box in any direction. The computer uses the inadequacies of the human mechanism of balance (located in the inner ear) to trick the body into believing it is experiencing all the sensations of flight – accelerating, turning, climbing, descending. The inner ear becomes confused if, for example, one tries to fly an aircraft in cloud without instruments. There are two reasons for this: first, in flight, gravity ('g' forces) can be distorted, and, secondly, the human mechanism is adaptive. Obviously gravity, which normally acts downwards towards the earth's centre, is the main reference for balance, but the inner ear can quickly adapt to changes. Spin around a few times, and, when you stop, the room feels as if it is rotating: your balance system has adapted to the spin, and is now trying to get back to normal.

The rams make use of this same effect. Pull the stick back to pitch up and a ram will move the front of the box upward, producing the expected increase in 'g'. Momentarily, you feel a little heavier. Adaptation starts right away, so the ram will slow down but produce the same effect. Return the stick to neutral and the ram stops. Your 'aircraft' pitch change may have been 10 degrees – the box may only have gone up 3 or 4 degrees. If you hold the new pitch attitude, the ram will slowly return the box itself to the level – slowly enough to avoid detection by your balance system. Watched from outside, the box is continuously in motion – small, jerky movements which it is hard to imagine producing the required result. The box does not go anywhere – it remains firmly attached to the floor – but the crew do: thousands of miles across the earth, and tens of thousands of feet up or down.

Should the motion system go berserk (and, like any device controlled by a computer, it can), the motions produced could be dangerous, so there is a 'panic button' on the flight deck, which simply cuts off all power and locks the simulator in position. The return to reality for the crew, if this happens, is a little precarious – the box can be canted up at some unhappy angle, and the floor is a long way below.

The simulator is nevertheless a welcome change from the classroom. Here at last one can start to get to grips with the real thing: sixteen four-hour flight periods, building up in complexity, to ensure that everything has been covered once, and most things many times. The first session is fairly gentle. All the checking routines, by now quite familiar, are rehearsed slowly, leading up to engine starting. There are no passengers, no real fuel is being burned, so stops can be made to repeat or explain. Taxying out for the first time, one appears to be on a real airfield. In fact a small TV camera is moving, in response to the pilot's movements, over a miniature landscape – a railway modeller's dream, complete with trees, grass, roads, even runway lights – mounted vertically on a wall in a separate room, as brightly lit as a film studio.

The instructor acts as the air traffic controller, answering requests for taxi and take-off clearance, to complete the sense of reality. Then comes the first take-off, followed by a climb up to 15,000 feet. After the leisurely start, the real-time activity of the take-off comes with a bit of a rush. But it is satisfying, too; after all, the machine is behaving very much like an aeroplane, even like other aeroplanes. And the take-off has gone quite well, too: speed schedules seem to be easy enough to achieve, it responds well to the controls – feels rather good, in fact. And it certainly goes up quickly, even at heavy weight.

At last the dusty tension of the classroom disappears. This, although a very different aeroplane, is a great deal more familiar than a desk covered with manuals. The appetite for flying returns. Level at 15,000 feet, the aeroplane is taken above the maximum permitted speed (to demonstrate the automatic neutralization of the outer elevons) and brought back again into the flight envelope; then a series of turns, with and without the autothrottles, to get the feel of the aircraft and observe the effect of power changes.

At this point, unreality returns briefly. It is time to start practising approaches to land, so the instructor dials into his console a reduction in weight – getting rid, in a few seconds, of the fuel which would have been burned during the cruise. Some more flying follows, deliberately looking at the effects of the autothrottle. Then the relationship between speed, angle of attack and power are explored, and the pilot begins to train himself to look at the angle of attack instrument, to include it in the regular scan pattern which sucks information from the cluster of dials in front of him.

Finally, he practises some approaches and landings – simple ones, with help from the ILS so that he can get used to the odd runway picture. The actual landings are the least satisfactory part of the Concorde simulator – not realistic enough to permit teaching of the finer points. But it is a truism of flying that nine-tenths of a good landing happen on the approach – getting the aeroplane into the proper position: 'the groove'. So the practice approaches are helpful.

Taxying in and the final shut-down checks complete the first session. Painless. Pleasant. Fun, even – but the crew have hardly begun. They have not been supersonic. There have been no failures. The flight engineer has practised some of his normal duties, including a partial fuel transfer, and is becoming used to taking more part in monitoring the pilots' flying. He is probably still getting a little tangled up with his powered seat. In spite of the simplicity of the exercise, all three will be feeling as if they have had a good workout.

In their next session the crew go supersonic for the first time. The flight engineer carries out the full fuel transfer, both ways. They start to learn to include the centre of gravity in their scan, and to check constantly that it is in the right place. The pilots explore the trim changes around Mach 1, the feel of turns at Mach 2, and they begin to learn to use the autopilot – this last being a surprisingly difficult task for some.

The whole generation of civil aircraft produced in the 1970s – the 747, the DC10, the L-1011 and Concorde – incorporated massive advances in automation. Their predecessors used autopilots extensively, some even being capable of automatic landing, but the functions performed were generally seen as assistance to the pilots in various phases of flight. The design of the new aircraft, however, put together functions such as autothrottles, automatic landing, navigation, altitude capture and warnings of deviation, to form a complete system around which all the flight procedures were based. Pilots who had spent perhaps ten years flying a 707 or VC10 and whose early training had been on aircraft without autopilots at all tended to feel that their arms and legs were the most reliable means of control. 'When in doubt, disengage everything and *fly* it,' was their approach, learned the hard way over many years. Now, suddenly, there were seventeen autopilot and three autothrottle modes to be used in an apparently infinite series of combinations – a whole new game.

Some pilots found the transition harder to make than anyone expected; some of those who made it still felt a little resentful of this intrusion on their skills. Any pilot who has driven an airliner down towards a runway on a dark night, in snow or sandstorm, can understand why. Inability to adapt to the automation was the principal cause of failure for those few who didn't make the grade.

All this may make it appear that Concorde's (and its contemporaries') automatics are some sort of technological nightmare, conjured up to injure pilotly pride. Not so – they are there to make flying safer. Most pilots learn the techniques quickly and find it satisfying to apply them. They still have to be able to fly the aircraft themselves – the automation simply extends the range of their own abilities.

Because of its central part in the aeroplane's procedures, learning the automatic way of flying becomes part of every simulator session after the first. The second exercise takes the crew supersonic. The third introduces flying with no auto-stabilization at Mach 2. Removing the smoothing effect of this system tends to cause over-control, leading to 'pilot-induced oscillations' of 1 to 2 degrees in amplitude – easy enough to cope with by simply returning the stick to neutral, which stops the motion, and then trying again more gently.

From here on, each session introduces more failures, concerning, for example, extreme angles of attack (which bring on the stick shaker and wobbler – the equivalent of stalls on other aircraft), the engines, the centre-of-gravity and flight control systems. In the eighth session there is an engine failure at Mach 2. Amazingly undramatic, but remember the wrong-way roll? The instructor makes a magic restoration of the failed engine and then fails two – on the same side. That's a little more interesting, but still quite containable. This is followed by several landings with three engines working.

Things are beginning to warm up, and the course is halfway through. Every conceivable failure is practised, every drill perfected. Gradually, in spite of this preoccupation with failures, familiarity with the normal operations builds up and confidence grows. The eleventh session reverses the crew's roles: the pilots operate the flight engineer's panel while he learns the landing procedures in the co-pilot's seat. Then two-engined landings start. No four-engined airliner is fun to fly on two, but all aircrew regularly train for this situation. Concorde on two engines is easier to fly than some, and the reserve of power available with afterburner is comforting, but it's still hard work.

The last three sessions concentrate on practical flying: using the automatic systems, recovering from deliberately induced errors, and encouraging each crew member to fill his place in the team. At the end they practise automatic landings in fog, which can be accurately reproduced at various levels of visibility by the simulator's visual system. Failures of ground and aircraft equipment are introduced, the fog thickens suddenly as in real life, 'go-arounds' are carried out from 100 feet, from just before the landing, even from after touch-down. (Go-arounds are aborted landings. They involve climbing away on a specified track from any height on approach, should, for example, the runway become blocked.)

Having survived all this, the crew know that they have wrung the aeroplane out thoroughly. They have experienced perhaps ten, perhaps a hundred times as many failures as will be contained in a lifetime of aviation. Flying the aircraft itself will be comparatively easy.

Flight Training

Flight training starts with looking at the aeroplane: touching it, prodding it, finding exactly where everything is, inspecting the mechanisms. Then up the steps, and a left turn into the tunnel which leads to the flight deck. There is a faint but noticeable resinous smell. Every aircraft has a characteristic aroma – a mixture of metal, rubber and kerosene – but the additional, slightly heady scent comes from the fibreglass ducting for the airconditioning system. Everything on the flight deck is by now familiar. The crew settle in, with an instructor in one of the pilots' seats (this is not a simulator – he cannot press the 'problem freeze' button). The eight hours of flight training get under way. This time is spent almost entirely on work within the airfield circuit – take-offs, approaches and landings, by day and night.

Three- and two-engined landings are practised again, with the 'failed' engines idling – much easier on the aircraft than on the simulator, with the full array of visual cues from the real world outside to help. Landings without autothrottle, without the radio altimeter, with the nose at 5 degrees (blanking out most of the view of the runway), with no visual or instrument glide slope guidance, with a supposedly incapacitated co-pilot – all are practised and perfected. This period ends with a competency check and a test for the renewal of the pilot's instrument rating. The aircrew licence can now be endorsed under the section 'Pilot in Command' with the coveted word 'Concorde'. But it is not over yet.

Route Supervision

Since the beginning of the course, three to four months ago, the flight crews have been brought back, step by step, to the real world, and now they are on their familiar territory, the route. They meet the cabin crew, who themselves have been through their version of the simulator – the cabin mock-up – which is an exact replica of the aircraft interior, including seats and galleys. Many of them are old friends from other fleets, other years.

Still with an instructor for the first few trips, they experience their first real supersonic flights. It may seem odd that this is not done during the period of training on the aircraft, but, in fact, the simulator is by far the best place to learn how the aeroplane behaves above Mach 1 – aircraft training time is much more efficiently used on low-level work. They begin now to learn the tricks peculiar to getting Concorde away on time, to fitting it into the air traffic control system, to the special qualities of each of the routes – to the day-to-day business of putting the aeroplane to work. Seven round trips are done in this way – fourteen sectors – before each captain, first officer and flight engineer are qualified to fly passengers unsupervised.

Inserted one at a time into fully trained crews, they spend the best part of two months on this phase. By the time it is over they are more comprehensively trained than any flight crew has ever been, and they are very ready to be let loose from the system – to get on with the job.

Routine Training

Three months after being checked out, each crewman returns to the simulator for a further look at his competency. After this, the regular routine applies: two-day checks on the simulator every six months, and an annual check on a scheduled flight. The six-monthly checks examine skills and re-train emergency procedures. The route check tests ability to operate under normal, real-world conditions.

The airline business depends very heavily on this continual process of training and checking. Improvements in crew training, as much as in aircraft reliability and flying techniques, have contributed to the high level of modern airline safety. The apparent obsession, in training exercises, with recovery from failures is easily justified by the fact that real failures happen so rarely nowadays. For example, an airline pilot would be unlucky if he experienced more than a single engine failure in a period of three years. For that very reason, he probably practises 30.

The six-monthly checks are, of course, tests to validate the licence, as well as opportunities for re-training. It is this feature which makes an airline pilot's life rather different from most. Not many people have to put their skills up for a thorough inspection so often: nor do they have to endure the nagging feeling that their job depends on a successful performance each time. One learns to live with it, but most airline families will agree that for a few days before each check the household atmosphere changes; tension builds up, manuals are spread out, part of the mind is increasingly somewhere else. An outsider might be forgiven for thinking it was all a little mad. Surely an experienced pilot, who has done it all so many times before, can take a little thing like a *simulator* check in his stride? But it is not just a question of passing the test – self-esteem needs to be refreshed.

To fly successfully is to execute a neat balancing act between over- and under-confidence. People who are honest with themselves (and those who aren't do not generally stay in the business very long) cannot avoid seeing their own mistakes. There are no ifs and buts: nobody else can be blamed. The simulator can even play back sections of the flight, reproducing faithfully the result of any ham-fistedness. So there is only one way to pass each check – as well as possible, so as to prove to oneself that the ability is still there.

The public is presented with a wonderfully distorted picture of the airline pilot. Lean, tanned, steely-eyed, he drives a sports car to work, briefly decorates an aeroplane which flies him automatically to his destination where he divides his time between a swimming pool and fornication. Actually, he is in the job because flying is habit-forming. The fact that it pays rather well merely reinforces the habit. The stewardesses drive the sports cars.

6. Flying Concorde

Driving to Heathrow Airport after an interval at home, my aircrew skin slowly regrows. Arriving from the west, as I do, I begin to notice aircraft, climbing out if the wind is westerly, or approaching to land if it is in the east. The weather changes its significance. No longer does it mean that the lawn need be watered, or the cabbages protected from frost. What matters now is the nature of the air – volatile or stable; the type of cloud – towering or layered. Clues begin to assemble, and, from long practice, a picture forms of the kind of flying weather in which the take-off will be flown.

Turning into the airport, an impression begins to form of how congested it will be. Sunday mornings are the worst: the largest number of departures, and crowds arriving to watch them leave. Passengers may be held up, the departure hall will be in tumult and the check-in staff will be under pressure. The mind begins to review the rest of the web of influences on any flight. Will the baggage loaders be 'working to rule'? Is there a fuel strike? A security scare?

Which particular aircraft will it be? Alpha Echo recently had an intermittent gauge in number nine fuel tank. One of Alpha Foxtrot's toilets developed a mind of its own on the last flight and flushed when least expected. The aircrew follow the ills, major and minor, of each of the aeroplanes with a sort of vicarious hypochondria.

Preparation

One and a half hours before departure the crew assembles at the operations office. Captain, first officer and flight engineer, they begin by reading the new flight notices – warnings of any changes that have not yet reached the manuals they all keep.

They will all know each other. In a small group like theirs, numbering less than a hundred, they may have trained on the same course. They are not a permanent crew. Each trip, originating and ending at the base airfield, is flown by a random grouping whose composition depends on the result of bids by each of them for that month's work. Most airlines feel that, apart from the administrative difficulties involved in 'crewing up', the needs of airline flying dictate that crew members should be mixed up in this way. High levels of safety demand consistency – a crew which flies together permanently can be very good, or it can become slack and develop bad habits.

Coming, as it were, fresh to each other, members of this particular crew will have to rely on the common standards to which they have been trained. They will probably remind themselves of the last time they flew together. Their conversation, during this brief period before the day's work starts, will be mainly about flying, completing the transition from home to aeroplane, turning the individuals into a crew.

Next, the briefing and flight plan. The briefing consists of a study of the state of navigational aids, radio communications and airfields along the routes. Collected by the States' Aeronautical Information Services, it is mostly about facilities that are temporarily off the air, and about work on airports which may have closed off sections of runways and taxiways. The necessarily dull text is sometimes enlivened by statements like 'pilots are advised to taxi with caution . . .' which makes one wonder what the writers think we usually do. Then, on to the weather.

The airport meteorological office provides a folder of weather information for every flight. Each one contains route forecast charts which depict the pressure systems, winds, temperatures, areas of possible turbulence and places where icing may be expected. From these forecasts are picked off all the pieces of information which will affect the flight plan. They also provide a useful general view of the kind of weather one is liable to encounter. Included with them are sheets of airport forecasts for all the airfields along the route. Aviation forecasts differ from the kind we can see daily on the TV screen in that they concentrate on what is important for flying. They come in a standard coded format. For example,

TAF
CYQX 0505 34015/25 3200 51DZ 10BR 3ST002 8ST008
INTER 0510 0800 51DZ 45FG 9//002 15 HR 34015/35 9999
3ST008 6SC015 INTER 3200 50DZ 10BR 8ST008

means:

Terminal Airfield Forecast (TAF) for Gander, Newfoundland (CYQX in the international four-letter airfield code), from 0500 GMT today until the same time tomorrow, is: wind from 340 degrees at 15 knots, gusting to 25 knots; visibility 3200 metres; drizzle and mist (the numbers here are detailed categories – the abbreviation BR is for the French *brume*, or mist); three-eighths of stratus cloud at 200 feet, with full cover at 800 feet. Intermittently, between 0500 and 1000 GMT, the visibility will drop to 800 metres in drizzle and fog and the sky will be obscured, with a vertical visibility of 200 feet (9//002). By 1500 GMT the gusts will have increased to 35 knots, the visibility will be better than 10 kilometres (9999) and the cloud will have lifted to three-eighths at 800 feet, with a second layer of six-eighths of stratocumulus at 1500 feet. In the same, later, period there will be, intermittently, a visibility of 3200 metres in drizzle and mist, and full cloud cover at 800 feet.

This may seem a somewhat complicated way of saying that it will be a damp, foggy night with an improvement expected in the morning, but it is full of information useful for the pilot. The surface chart shows that at the time of the poorer weather the airfield was under the back end of a frontal system which had already passed out into the Atlantic. Its passage is confirmed by the steady wind direction – in the northern hemisphere, the wind always veers after a front has gone through. At 1400 GMT, when we expect to be closest to Gander, the improvement will have started, and the conditions should be within our landing limits. Acceptable, but not cause for celebration – the sort of weather that we'll watch closely during the flight, following trends in the half-hourly radio broadcasts.

Also included in the folder are observations of the actual weather, usually taken hourly. These are perhaps as useful as the forecasts, as the short flight time makes them quite relevant. Certainly the crew will pay particular attention to them in weather broadcasts received during the flight. For Concorde flights, the staff at the destination airport send a 'PREDEPMET' message over the airline's communication system. It arrives at briefing time and includes their own summary of the weather and the state of the airfield navigation aids. This is more immediate than the international state system, and has the human advantage that if it is inaccurate the captain can express his feelings about it to the sender at the end of the flight.

The briefing completed, the crew turn their attention to the flight plan, whose main purpose is to determine the amount of fuel required for this particular flight. The routes over which the aircraft flies are predetermined, but they can vary enormously in nature, and the conditions are different from day to day. The route from London to Bahrain (the first one we flew), for example, starts with a long subsonic portion over Europe, as far as Venice.

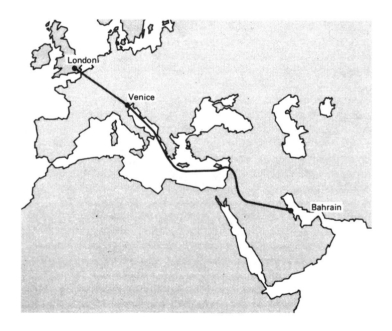

Thereafter, the climb and acceleration begin down the Adriatic Sea, and Mach 2 is maintained all the way until the descent into Bahrain. In vertical cross-section the flight looks like this:

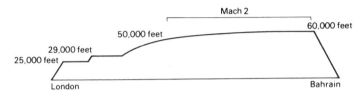

The picture on the return journey is the opposite:

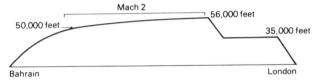

In both cases, the winds at the lower altitudes can have a significant effect on times and therefore on the fuel load.

The North Atlantic routes to New York and Washington involve short subsonic segments at both ends of the flight where the aircraft is overland.

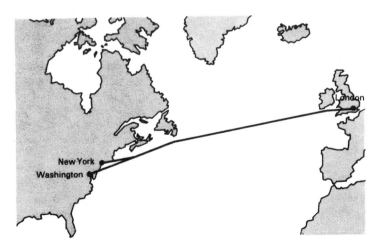

Reaching a rather lower maximum altitude, and with descent steps in US airspace, the cross-sections are a little more complex:

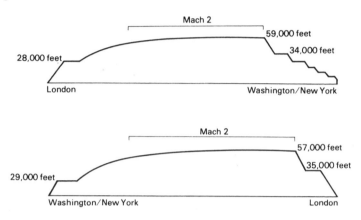

The winds at subsonic levels have less effect on these routes but the air is comparatively warm and temperature variations are important.

Given fixed route lengths: 3500 miles to New York, 3780 to Washington and 3730 to Bahrain, the variables in the fuel calculation are the wind components (head or tail wind), the temperature at supersonic levels (affecting the efficiency of the engines – generally speaking, the colder the better), and the aircraft's weight (affected by the payload). Reserves of fuel against the possibility of diversion and holding have to be there at the end of the flight, so they are added to the landing weight for the purpose of estimating the 'trip fuel' – the fuel that will actually be burned during the flight. To these two quantities – the trip fuel and the fuel for diversion and holding – is added a fixed amount for en route contingencies such as errors in weather forecasting. The total of the three is the 'flight plan fuel' – a minimum without which no flight can depart.

On a typical flight, this is likely to be within the range of 75 to 95 tons. As 95 tons is the maximum tank capacity, there is sometimes room for further fuel. Occasionally, it is sensible to take some of it. For example, there may be known delays at the destination airfield, the weather may be of the sort that can close an airfield for short periods, or there may be a long line of aircraft at the take-off point.

This planning process for each flight serves a psychological as well as a mechanical purpose. It makes the crew think in detail about the circumstances surrounding the coming flight, and allows them to prepare themselves mentally for all the likely variations. They will, for example, look into the case of what to do if an engine fails in the cruise. The actual business of coping with the failure is something they can do almost in their sleep, they have practised it so often. But Concorde needs all four of its engines to maintain supersonic flight, and with one failed it has to descend and fly subsonically. In doing so it becomes less efficient, and its range is reduced by about a quarter. For most

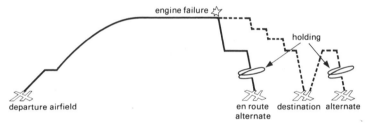

of the flight it is possible, in this event, to return to the departure airfield or to continue to the destination, but within a section in the middle it is not. So 'en route alternate' airfields are studied and a small chart prepared, showing exactly where one can go from various points along the track. Some airfields which serve this purpose on the North Atlantic route are Shannon, Eire; Santa Maria in the Azores; Gander, Newfoundland; and Halifax, Nova Scotia.

One further subject is looked into at this stage: the balance, or trim, of the aircraft. The need to position the centre of gravity accurately for take-off, and to allow room in the trim tanks for fuel to be shifted in flight to redistribute the weight, makes this a more complicated process than on most aircraft. The fact that almost all the passengers sit in front of the centre of gravity means that allowance must be made for the possibility that some will not show for the flight. Fuel will be burned during the taxi, so at high loads that fuel is put in the rear trim tank, in order that, when it has been used, space is freed for transfer later on. It is an interesting game, getting the trim right on Concorde, and the loading officers, in combination with the flight planners and the crews, have developed the ability to make very fine judgments.

By this time, the flight engineer has left to perform his external and internal checks on the aircraft and to supervise the fuelling. The two pilots, by now well familiar with the nature of the coming flight, clip their copies of the flight plan, en route chart and flight log (which carries all the data concerning the waypoints, altitudes and radio frequencies – a sort of work sheet) to their flight boards, and set off to join him on the flight deck. Negotiating security guards, puddles of unidentifiable fluid and trains of baggage carts, they approach the aircraft, which looks a little tail-heavy with the weight of fuel already on board, surrounded by vehicles full of bags, food and drink, and connected by umbilical cords to electrical power, airconditioning and fuel trucks.

Starting

Let us assume that today's flight is the BA 193 to New York: departure time, 11.15 am. It is now 10.15 and the crew are beginning their checks. The inertial navigation systems need to be started up and told where they are, maps and charts have to be selected, the speeds for the take-off worked out, and the departure procedure studied. Each of the three crew check a part of the instrument panels and set them up for flight. They do this part of the preparation not from a checklist but from a memorized scanning sequence. Gradually the systems come to life. Heads are down, arms reaching out, gongs ringing, lights flashing as the warnings are checked.

The cabin crew, six of them, have had their own briefing and know, among other things, which passengers have requested particular seats, who has asked for special meals, and whether there are any children or elderly passengers booked. They have probably recognized the names of regular travellers, some of whom may be important businessmen or women, government ministers, diplomats or stars of the entertainment and sporting world. They will also know if any passengers have connections to make, and if anyone has been what is euphemistically known as 'mishandled'. (This usually means that their baggage has been sent to the wrong destination on some previous flight – not necessarily, or even probably, on Concorde. But the story can be much worse. When the airline system breaks down it can do so in a big way.) The cabin crews are adept at giving special attention to those who need it. Even very distinguished figures can be nervous on an aeroplane; patience and charm help a great deal to restore their confidence.

While doing their own preparation, the cabin crew will usually find time to deliver some tea or coffee to the flight deck where by now, about half an hour before departure, the captain will be briefing the crew for the take-off. An extraordinary ritual, this, one might think: two grown men listening intently to a recital by the third of the whole of the take-off and climb-out they are about to perform. 'The co-pilot will call, "Speed building, 100 knots, V_1, rotate and V_2." At 100 knots we shall require at least three afterburners operative. The engineer will call, "Power checked" or "Engine failure" . . .' And so on, covering every moment of the departure. As well as serving the practical purposes of rehearsing the activities to come and of bringing out any unusual features which might apply on a particular day, the take-off briefing serves to re-establish the common ground between the individual crewmen – their training and accumulated knowledge of the aircraft and the airfield.

Twenty minutes before departure, the fuelling is complete and the passengers are boarding, their coats having preceded them, on wheeled racks, to be put away in cupboards. The loadsheet arrives and is checked carefully. This document, printed out from a computer, is the final summary of the weight and balance of the aircraft. By now the exact number of passengers and the weight of baggage is known, as is their distribution. The computation ensures that the total weight of the aeroplane (up to 185 tons) is within limits for take-off, and that the weight on landing will also be suitable. The centre of gravity is checked. The total fuel on board is confirmed, and the captain signs the loadsheet. The passengers now on board, the ramp coordinator makes his final report to the cockpit and leaves the aircraft, closing the door behind him.

'ASI bugs and pitch index . . .'

'Checked.'

Movable white markers on the air-speed indicators have been set to the take-off speeds, and pitch angle indices in the attitude instruments (controlled by thumbwheels on the control columns) have been positioned at the calculated angle for the climb-out.

'Clock, engine and TLA bugs . . .'

'Checked.'

There will be a power reduction at a predetermined time after the start of the take-off roll, to a calculated power setting. The clock-timer and throttle lever angle markers are set up. During the take-off a monitoring system will watch the engine power. The minimum acceptable settings for this take-off are dialled into the instruments.

'Start clearance . . .'

The co-pilot calls air traffic control for permission to start the engines.

'London Ground, Speedbird Concorde 193 on stand Juliet Two for start-up?'

'Speedbird Concorde 193, clear to start. Call on 121.9 for pushback.'

A few final items of the before-start checklist are gone through, and then number three engine starts to wind up. Stretch in the seat a little, here. It is three minutes to the scheduled departure time, a glance down the aisle shows that the passengers are seated (some already have their morning papers open), and we will shortly be under our own power. As for the crew, we have re-entered that private world where decisions are reasonably clear-cut, problems are known and understood – where we need rely only on ourselves. It is a marvellous feeling, this sense of independence. The awesome responsibility makes flying of this kind no light-hearted business, but the atmosphere on the flight deck is exhilarating, backed as it is by a respectful confidence in one's own and one's crew's abilities.

While the flight engineer starts the second engine, the captain makes an announcement to the passengers, outlining, for the benefit of those who have not flown on the aircraft before, what will happen on take-off. This is necessary because the extraordinary power makes the whole of the take-off a rather more sporting affair than usual – pleasant if expected, but possibly a little alarming if not.

The aeroplane is pushed backwards by a tug into the centre of the tarmac, where the remaining two engines are started. All aircraft have to do this in certain parts of Heathrow, to keep the noise to tolerable levels for the ground crews. Hydraulic power is now available from the engine-driven pumps, so the flying controls are checked. Another sequence of calls and responses from the checklist prepares the aircraft for taxying. When all four engines are running, the ground engineer removes his intercom plug and disconnects the tug. Before the aircraft moves away, the nose and visor are lowered to the 5-degree position. There is a 'clunk' as the uplocks release, and another as the mechanism locks the nose down.

Taxying

Sitting on the flight deck as the aircraft taxies, no one could mistake the motion for anything but Concorde's. The long, narrow fuselage produces a springiness which can be felt as far back as the first few rows of cabin seats. From the rear of the cabin, looking forward, the effect is quite obvious: you can see the fuselage flex as the nosewheel runs over bumps. This flexibility is not weakness – an aircraft's structural strength depends partly on its ability to take up shocks in this way.

No more than idle power is needed to keep it moving. In fact, it has to be braked occasionally to prevent it from gathering speed. Steering is effected through a small handle on the side panel. The pilot is 38 feet ahead of the nosewheel and 97 feet in front of the main wheels, so keeping it to the centre of a taxiway at a junction can sometimes involve the cockpit travelling over the grass for part of the turn.

During the taxi, another 30 checks are made, most by the flight engineer, on the aircraft systems. Fuel is pumped forward from the rear trim tank for use before take-off, and passengers may hear the whine of the electrical pumps running. They may also notice the reverse thrust being tested briefly.

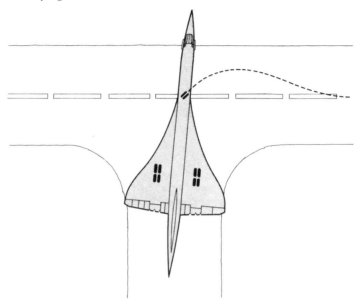

Departure clearance is received. Take-off is on runway 28R, the northern of the two parallel runways whose take-off direction is 277 degrees Magnetic. The route will be a Standard Instrument Departure (SID) towards Brecon, the 'Brecon One Foxtrot'. This means a climb-out straight ahead, until picking up a track of 263 degrees from a radio beacon just north of the airfield, then flying that track until seven miles from the same beacon, where a right turn is required on to a track of 275 degrees to Woodley, near Reading. Woodley must be crossed at or above 4000 feet altitude, and clearance to climb is restricted to 6000 feet for the time being. Speed must be no more than 250 knots (290 mph), and a radio frequency of 132.8 mHz will be used by the departure controller after take-off. We shall be superimposing on this our anti-noise procedure, which will involve cutting back the power at one minute and eleven seconds after the start of the roll, and re-applying it gradually between 5000 and 8000 feet on the climb.

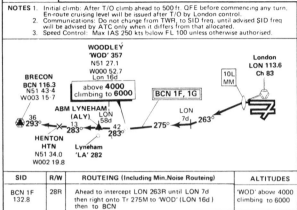

| Trans alt **6000** | | | **BRECON SID**s |

NOTES 1. Initial climb: After T/O climb ahead to 500 ft. QFE before commencing any turn. En-route cruising level will be issued after T/O by London control.
2. Communications: Do not change from TWR, to SID freq. until advised SID freq will be advised by ATC only when it differs from that allocated.
3. Speed Control: Max IAS 250 kts below FL 100 unless otherwise authorised.

WOODLEY
'WOD' 357
N51 27.1
W000 52.7
Lon 16d

London
LON 113.6
Ch 83

BRECON
BCN 116.3
N51 43·4
W003 15·7

above **4000**
climbing to **6000**

10L
MM

BCN 1F, 1G

ABM LYNEHAM
(ALY)   LON
58d

LON
7d   263°

36
293°   13
283°   42
283°   275°

HENTON
HTN
N51 34.0
W002 19.8

Lyneham
'LA' 282

SID	R/W	ROUTEING (Including Min.Noise Routeing)	ALTITUDES
BCN 1F 132.8	28R	Ahead to intercept LON 263R until LON 7d then right onto Tr 275M to 'WOD' (LON 16d) then to BCN	'WOD' above 4000 climbing to 6000

Standard Instrument Departure

We have now arrived at the holding point, where we await our turn to go. This is an opportunity for a quick review of the situation. All the checks, except the final ones, which will be done as we move on to the runway, are now complete. The aeroplane is properly balanced, the flight engineer has moved his seat forward, having set his systems up to take care of themselves, and the cabin service officer has reported that the cabin is prepared for take-off. When cleared, we taxi on to the runway and line up, checking the sky ahead for aircraft and weather – radar on, if necessary. We're ready to go as soon as the control tower gives the word.

'Speedbird Concorde 193, cleared for take-off.'

'193 rolling.'

The Take-off

'Three, two, one, now.'

The two pilots' clock-timers, which will count down to zero at the cut-back, are started as the throttles go fully forward. There is an almost immediate push in the back as we set off down the runway.

'Airspeed building –'

The co-pilot has checked both indicators. The afterburners begin to come in, speeding up the acceleration. Out of the corner of the eye, the green lights are seen to come on as the engines get enough air to develop full power and the afterburners light up.

'100 knots.'

'Power checked.'

Now we are really beginning to move, and a little work on the rudder pedals keeps us straight.

'V_1.'

V_1, the decision speed, is 165 knots today. Up to this point we would be able to stop on the runway if, say, an engine failed. From here on, any failure will be taken into the air. The right hand moves from the throttles to the stick. The airspeed needle is approaching the next bug, set at 192 knots.

'Rotate.'

A fairly sharp initial backward movement of the stick gets the nose moving upwards. Eased off a little, this turns into a gentle rotation up to the preset pitch angle of $13\frac{1}{2}$ degrees. The rotation should take between five and six seconds. At an angle of 10 degrees and a speed of 205 knots the wheels leave the ground. Reaching $13\frac{1}{2}$ degrees, the aircraft is held there while the speed builds up.

'V_2.'

221 knots – a safe flying speed, even with an engine failed.

'240 knots.'

Speed is rapidly building up towards the required 250 knots, so a gentle pitch up is started, to about 18 degrees, to contain it.

'Three, two, one, noise.'

Cut-back time. The afterburners are switched off, and the throttles brought crisply back to their new setting. Anticipating the cut-back, the pitch angle is reduced to about 12 degrees. At 250 knots, we are now climbing at about 1000 feet per minute as we pass over the houses closest to the airport. Our height is about 2000 feet.

With the nose and visor lowered, it is quite noisy on the flight deck. We intercept the 263 degrees track, then at 7 miles turn right again, looking for the 4000-foot altitude that will keep us clear of light aircraft crossing below at Woodley.

As soon as that altitude is reached, and with clearance from the departure controller, we begin to speed up. From 5000 feet the power starts to go on. Further clearance is given to climb. By 8000 feet, a little to the west of Reading, we are at full power again and getting close to our proper climb-speed of 400 knots. The nose and visor have been raised, and we are climbing at about 3000 feet per minute, cleared now to 28,000 feet. The autopilot is engaged and instructed to take us to the cleared altitude at climb speed. The autothrottles are primed, ready to take power off when we reach our cruise height. The INS is now in charge of navigation, taking us to the pre-programmed way-points: Lyneham in Wiltshire next, then to the acceleration point in the Bristol Channel.

This is always a pleasant point in the flight. Take-off is a period of pretty concentrated activity, making sure the anti-noise procedure and the SID are done correctly. The departure controller is on his toes, too. His job is to shepherd climbing aircraft through the pattern of those inbound, keeping them apart with instructions to turn (vectors), and with control of altitude. Getting settled in the climb is the first break in total concentration since the start of take-off. There is now time to think more generally. How are the passengers? Can we turn off the seat-belt sign? What is the weather like ahead? Is our oceanic clearance confirmed?

The Subsonic Cruise

At 28,000 feet we cruise at Mach ·95 – just below the speed of sound. The interlude has been a short one because we are now approaching the acceleration point. The oceanic clearance has come through – to climb when ready and cruise between 50,000 and 60,000 feet on track Sierra November, the northernmost of the three fixed SST tracks across the North Atlantic. London Airways has given us clearance to climb under their radar control which, through remote stations, reaches well out to the south-west of Eire.

We may still be in cloud and there can be turbulence here, but the aeroplane rides it well – the wings, although narrow in span, have a large area. Compared with most jets, the wing loading is low, so gusts are well-cushioned. A short transonic checklist is carried out and the fuel transfer started – from the forward trim tanks to the rear – preparing for the change to supersonic flight. A brief explanation to the passengers lets them know what is coming. Many of them will want to see the figure 1 appear in the cabin Machmeters.

The Acceleration

The throttles are moved fully forward again, for full power. They will stay there until we decelerate on the other side of the ocean. The afterburners are re-lit, two at a time. They could all be switched on together, but the extra thrust coming on so suddenly would be uncomfortable. Selected in pairs, they produce two gentle nudges. The Mach number quickly increases through Mach 1. On the instrument panel, the precise moment at which the shock wave starts can be observed, as the altimeter and vertical speed indicator (both looking at pressure) go temporarily haywire. Once the wave has settled on the nose, only a few seconds later, they calm down. The aircraft is pitched up once more, to contain the speed, and it begins to climb. As it climbs, the Mach number continues to rise.

The 'sound barrier' no longer exists. Going through Mach 1 produces no shudder, no bump, no noise. On the contrary, the aeroplane seems to like it. It slides through the speed of sound and on up to higher speeds as if it had been waiting to be let off the leash. At Mach 1·3 the air intakes begin to work noticeably. Needles on four small gauges at the forward end of the flight engineer's panel show that the ramps are moving down to control the incoming air: to slow it down and compress it before it reaches the engine face. The temperature of the outside air begins to be very interesting: the hotter it is, the slower the climb will be, and the more fuel will be used.

Since the temperature falls off with height, it would be impossible to say whether a particular temperature was 'hot' or 'cold' unless there was something to compare it with. Aircraft use the 'international standard atmosphere' for this purpose. It assumes a steady fall in temperature from 15°C at sea level to −56°C at 36,500 feet, and constant temperature above that

1. Take-off: the beginning of the rotation from a wet runway; the nosewheel has just lifted off.

2. Landing: small trails of smoke from the tyres show that the wheels have just touched the runway and that this was a good landing. The attitude is right and the elevons are well back, indicating that the pilot has successfully countered the pitch-down tendency in the ground effect. The nose and visor have been lowered to the landing position.

4. The simulator's terrain: a small television camera mounted on the gantry is 'flown' by the pilot over the model. Day, night and any degree of fog can be represented.

3. The flight simulator at Filton: mounted on huge hydraulic jacks which can move it in any direction, it reacts to the pilot's control movements, while a picture of the terrain is projected on to the inside of the screen (top right).

5. Concorde at Mach 2: a rare photograph, taken from the liner QE2 in mid-Atlantic. (*Inset*) The cabin machmeter, reading twice the speed of sound—about 1350 mph.

6. The prototype flight deck: a large space on the centre instrument panel is reserved for a moving map display, and the flight engineer has his own set of throttles (bottom right).

7. The production flight deck: all the automatic flight controls are grouped together in the glareshield, and a full set of engine instruments faces the flight engineer when he turns his seat and moves it forward.

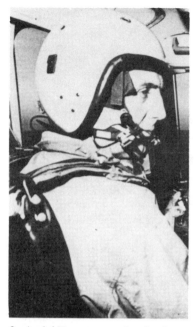 

8. André Turcat preparing for the first flight of 001.

9. Brian Trubshaw, in airline-style uniform.

10. 001 being towed out of its hangar at the roll-out ceremony, 11 December 1967.

11. Concorde takes off: 001 leaving the ground for the first time, at Toulouse-Blagnac on 2 March 1969.

12. 002 landing at Fairford at the end of its first flight, attended by its 'chase' Canberra.

13. The structural test specimen at Farnborough.

14. The fuel system test rig.

15. A tail section being loaded into a 'Super Guppy' at Filton for delivery to France.

16. De-icing trials: the aircraft is being flown into a trail of water discharged from the tanker ahead.

17. The prototype's tail parachute deployed after landing.

18. Simultaneous departure into airline service by British Airways (London to Bahrain) and Air France (Paris to Rio de Janeiro), as seen by television viewers on 21 January 1976.

19. (*Above*) The inaugural arrival in Washington DC on 24 May 1976: a burly security guard watches over the two aircraft parked nose-to-nose in front of Dulles Airport's control tower. (*Below*) Press conference in Washington: the author, surrounded.

20. Concorde lands at New York for the first time, 19 October 1977.

21. 201 adds a touch of dignity to the press conference at
John F. Kennedy Airport. At the table (left to right):
McKinlay, Dudal, Walpole, Franchi, Perrier.

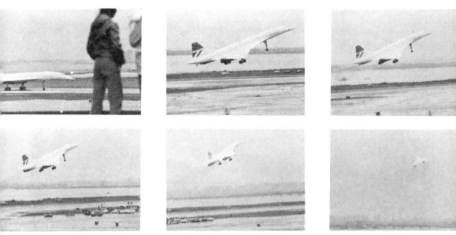

22. First departure from New York, 20 October 1977: 'It's a non-event.'

23. The same take-off, from the left-hand side: 201 shows its Air France colours. Queens, New York, is in the background.

24. 22 November 1977: the first airline flights arrive at New York.

25. Concorde takes its place among other British Airways airliners at JFK Airport, New York.

height. An instrument on the flight deck compares the actual air temperature with the ISA, and reads the difference. This 'temperature difference' (TD) is a very important figure.

We sometimes refer, then, to the outside air as being 'hot' when its temperature is − 50°C. This is not a sign of dementia, any more than is the apparently obvious statement that air at − 70°C is 'cold' – it is just a convenient way of expressing relatively the nature of the air we are flying in. Warm upper air is found fairly often during the climb between 40,000 and 50,000 feet, at about 10 degrees west longitude.

The climb route, slightly south of west in direction, passes about 45 miles from the coast of Eire at its closest point.

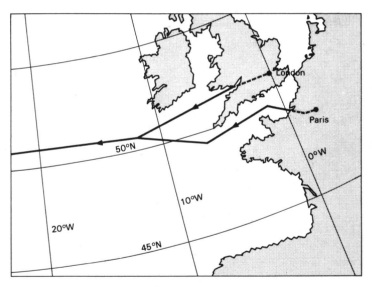

Departure routes

At longitude 12 degrees west, the track from Paris joins. There is normally no conflict between the British and French schedules, but if there is, one aircraft will be held up a few minutes on the ground to allow a separation in time at this point of 15 minutes – about 340 miles. Some time before this point, the afterburners will have been switched off: above Mach 1·7 they are no longer required, and a slower climb is continued up to Mach 2, at 50,000 feet, the start of the cruise.

The Cruise

The true airspeed from now on will be between 1300 and 1350 mph: about 22 miles per minute, or a mile every 2·7 seconds. The actual groundspeed may differ from this by up to 100 mph each way – slower westbound against the wind, and faster eastbound with the wind behind.

But in the aeroplane, one might as well be stationary. Ten miles above the earth, and three to four miles above the nearest cloud, there is nothing to give the eye a sense of movement. It takes a conscious effort to persuade oneself that the speed is real. A look at the INS groundspeed read-out shows it, but rather more convincing, for some reason, are the miles ticking by in the distance-to-go display. They reduce, obviously, as one approaches the next waypoint. The rate is impressive. In the time it takes to read this sentence, two miles go by.

The flight is usually remarkably smooth, becoming more so as the cruise progresses and the aircraft slowly climbs. Each of the fixed routes is used only by SSTs going in one direction, so the complete band of altitudes – between 50,000 and 60,000 feet – is available to them all. It is therefore possible to cruise in the most efficient way, at a fixed power, so that, as fuel is burned off and the weight decreases, the aircraft is allowed to climb. This technique, known as 'cruise climb', was used in the early jet era, when the subsonic airspace was also free. It had to be abandoned when the numbers of jet aircraft grew. For Concorde, which could also, if necessary, fly quite happily at fixed altitudes, it means a slight but worthwhile saving in fuel. On a North Atlantic crossing the aircraft will reach somewhere between 56,000 and 58,000 feet by the end of the cruise.

Lunch is being served. The long cabin, with its rather narrow central aisle, does not permit the flourishes that accompany first-class meals on subsonic aircraft. Nor is there time for the laying-up of individual place settings or the carving of joints of meat. But there has already been a cocktail service and there now follows a four-course meal: *hors d'oeuvres*, a choice of three *entrées* (one of them generally the much-demanded steak, with alternatives of fish and poultry), a dessert and cheese. Fine wines are served with the meal, and coffee and liqueurs follow. The food is well-chosen and presented, and always of high quality.

Of the six cabin staff, two work principally in the galleys, preparing and serving the food and drinks, while the other four attend to the passengers. Naturally, the business of getting as many as a hundred meals served demands a high degree of organization, and the cabin crew must be prepared to stop at any time to deal with the individual needs of a passenger, so they work hard during the flight. The job is physically taxing, too – because of the steep climb angle, getting loaded trolleys out of the rear galley is literally uphill work. Concorde needs, and seems to get, highly motivated people to work in its cabin. The cabin crews enjoy their job because they are able to do it well and because of the response they get from the passengers. After all, apart from Concorde, there are very few aircraft in the world that can fly at Mach 2 (and those are all military), probably none that can do so for two and a half hours without refuelling, and certainly none that can do all this while a hundred passengers are served with champagne, lobster and roast grouse.

On the flight deck, the crew is settled into the cruise. The autopilot is engaged, in the MAX CRUISE mode. At these heights the two limiting parameters are Mach number and skin temperature. If the outside air temperature is much above $-50°C$ $(ISA + 6°$ – on the hot side), we will be watching the nose temperature rise close to $127°C$, expecting the autopilot to reduce the Mach number when it is reached.

This is a time of lessened workload, even though we are moving so fast. The waypoints are spaced at 10-degree intervals of longitude, so there are reasonable time-intervals between them. At each one, however, a very thorough check has to be made. Is the next waypoint correct? Is the computer-defined track correct? Is the computer right about the distance between the two points? Do we need to enter any new points? What is the fuel remaining, and, with the fuel subtracted for the remaining flight, will the reserves be those calculated? When satisfied that all is as expected, the co-pilot sends a position report. Up to 30 degrees west longitude, the report goes to 'Shanwick' (a combination of Shannon and Prestwick), the Anglo-Irish control service for the eastern Atlantic area. Beyond 30 degrees west, control transfers to Gander.

The flight engineer, between checks of his systems, tunes in and copies down the weather broadcasts: Shannon (in case of return); Gander and Halifax in the Maritime provinces of Canada; Bangor, Maine; Hartford, Connecticut; Boston; New York; Newark; Baltimore; Philadelphia; and Washington. All these are places which we can reach and which are in some way prepared for a Concorde transit should the weather deteriorate at our destination. There are many other airfields which could accept us, but if a diversion is necessary, it helps to go somewhere where spares are held and where, if possible, the staff have had some experience of handling the aircraft.

Throughout the cruise, gentle activity is going on, scanning the instruments, checking, cross-checking, re-checking. The crew eat, too – an abbreviated version of the meal served to the passengers (without the wines, of course). There is a rule, followed by all airlines, that captains and co-pilots should always choose different dishes when they eat in the air, to guard against the remote possibility of food poisoning. We follow the rule on Concorde, too. It doesn't in the least diminish the pleasure of eating in the fastest restaurant in the world, with the best view.

The meal doesn't last long, though. It is soon time to start preparing for descent. Look for Newfoundland on the radar, selecting the 300-mile scale, tune in a DME station to provide the tightening-up for the navigation computers, get out the charts for the approach and landing, select the radio frequency for the message from our company which will tell us what the actual conditions are at New York.

We are running down past the Maritimes at 55,000 feet altitude, now, and the co-pilot is in contact with Moncton centre on VHF. It looks as if we shall end the cruise at about 56,000 feet today, and we check our descent distance. We shall need to be at 39,000 feet below Mach 1 at least 50 miles before Hyannis – 30 miles before we cross the coast at Cape Cod.

Allowing for a 50 mph headwind, we shall have to reduce power 132 miles before we want to reach Mach 1, 182 miles before Hyannis. Now follows a conference similar to that which

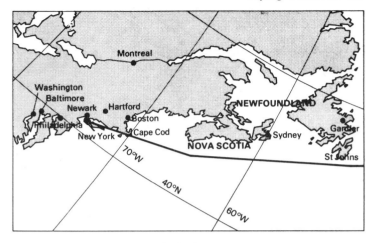

Arrival route

occurred before start-up at Heathrow, only this time the briefing is for the approach and landing at John F. Kennedy Airport, New York. The descent, the expected arrival route and runway, the type of approach, landing technique and the procedure for go-around are covered. This review complete, and descent clearance received from Boston centre, the captain tells the passengers that we are about to slow down. They will, most likely, still be drinking their coffee.

The Descent

Very, very gently, the throttles are brought back to a mid-position. While the autopilot holds the aircraft at the last cruise altitude, the Mach number drops quite rapidly. Suddenly we are reminded of what has kept us going so fast. At Mach 2, balanced, as it were, in the middle of the equation of thrust and drag, we were hardly aware of the four Olympus engines. Only now, by its absence, is their power demonstrated.

At Mach 1·6 the throttles are brought further back and the aircraft is pitched down to begin the descent, which is carried out at a constant indicated airspeed of 350 knots. Indicated airspeed (the speed shown on the pilots' instruments) is measured by comparing dynamic pressure, which depends on speed, with static pressure – that is, the pressure of the local air. Since pressure changes (reduces) with height, this is the only useful aerodynamic measure of speed, but it bears little relation to the actual, or true, airspeed once the aeroplane is substantially away from the earth's surface. At this point in the descent, for instance, the true airspeed is still around 1000 miles an hour.

During the descent the true airspeed and the Mach number continue to reduce. The distinctive hooked shape of Cape Cod stands out clearly on the radar. Progress along the descent slope is checked. This can be done from tables, but there is a useful rule-of-thumb which gives a quick answer: the figures behind the decimal point of the Mach number are roughly equal to the miles to go to Mach 1. Thus, at Mach 1·47, say, it will take about 47 miles for the Mach number to reduce to 1.

The descent rate will be around 5000 feet per minute, and so the autopilot will begin to capture the selected cruise altitude (usually 39,000 feet) early – some 2000 to 3000 feet above. A gentle pitch up starts, and the aircraft settles at its required height. Mach 1 is seen for the last time on the flight, the autothrottles are engaged, and once more the aeroplane is cruising at Mach ·95. From now on, although cruising some 15 per cent faster, we are back in the world of the subsonic jets, and will conform to all the same procedures.

The most attractive part of the flight is over: the stratospheric calm is behind us and the tempo is increasing. As we head from Hyannis on Cape Cod to Hampton on Long Island, we are transferred from Boston air traffic control centre to New York. Although this is a quiet time of day at Kennedy (it is now 9.30 am Eastern Standard Time), an airport which handles some 1300 aircraft movements a day is never dull. Radio communications become busy. We listen to the terminal information broadcast, and are likely to find the runway has been changed (a computer at Kennedy airport allocates landing and take-off runways in order to vary the noise patterns around the airport, and 9.00 am seems to be one of its favourite times to make a change).

Further descent clearance comes now, in steps, as we are

handed over from controller to controller. At 10,000 feet we slow to 250 knots, lowering the visor and nose. The angle of attack is about 6 degrees, and we begin to feel the vortex lift acting on the wing.

'Speedbird 193 heavy, you have crossing traffic at eleven o'clock, slow moving, north-west bound, altitude unknown.'

'Speedbird 193, looking.'

The controller has on his radar picture a 'blip' showing an aircraft flying, in visual conditions, quite legally across our path. He has judged its speed, and it is probably a light aircraft at low altitude, but three pairs of eyes will spend a good proportion of their time looking out for it. Unless it clears our path we may have to ask the controller to vector us around it.

To the European mind, accustomed to various forms of restriction, the freedom of the American skies can seem alarming. Put simply, the airspace below 10,000 feet in the USA is largely open to all aircraft as long as there is good enough visibility to see and be seen. Radar controllers provide information to those aircraft under their control (principally airliners), but cannot necessarily communicate with the smaller aircraft. The burden of avoidance seems to fall rather heavily, therefore, on the larger, faster aircraft.

One must remember, however, that the airspace over the USA is much less cluttered with military areas, and that in general the centres of dense traffic are further apart. Navigation aids and radar coverage are more advanced than they are in Europe as a whole, and the system clearly works. Statistically, the USA is still the safest part of the world in which to fly. The airliners, with very effective help from the controllers, can cope, and the light aircraft are as unrestricted as is reasonably possible. European airspace, hampered as it is by the need for much more extensive military reservation, and the fact that regulations vary from country to country, is a much less pleasant place for general aviation. In Britain in particular, getting from one place to another in a small aircraft can be something of an obstacle race.

'Cleared direct to Deer Park. Descend to 8000 feet. Leave Deer Park on the 221-degree radial for vectors to the three-one Left ILS. Change to Kennedy Approach . . .'

From the main entry point, north-east of the airfield, we will fly the standard route, slightly out to sea, and turn right on to the instrument approach to the left hand of the two parallel runways whose landing direction is 310 degrees magnetic.

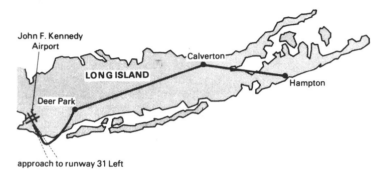

approach to runway 31 Left

A series of clearances arrive, allowing us to descend to 2500 feet over the water. Soon after crossing the coast the airspeed is further reduced in stages, so that when turning on to the final approach we will be at 190 knots (220 mph). As we have slowed down, so has the angle of attack increased to produce the necessary lift. By now, level at 2500 feet, it is 11 degrees. Already we have begun to adopt that predatory look.

The Final Approach

Lined up on the localizer, we see the runway ahead and watch for the bar which represents the glidepath to come down from the top of the instrument. As it does so, the wheels are selected down. Lights on the undercarriage indicator show that the doors have opened and that the up-locks have broken. A bump indicates that the nosewheel has come down. A green light confirms it is locked. Another for the tailwheel. Two more bumps for the main wheels. As one always arrives before the other, there is a slight sideways lurch in each direction – hard to feel in the cabin, but distinct on the flight deck.

'Four greens. Nose down.'

Now we need the nose fully drooped, to 12½ degrees. It becomes invisible, leaving a completely clear view of the territory ahead. The rest of the landing check is completed and we fly down the glideslope. At this point, say six miles from the runway threshold, and on the correct glideslope, the runway looks odd to a new Concorde pilot. The aircraft seems too high.

It always seems amazing that the eye can judge an approach at 3 degrees to the surface, but I suppose it is no more odd than the ability to aim a flexible golf club at a small stationary ball, or a tennis racket at a larger but moving one. To a pilot, on final approach, a runway looks like this:

If he is too low, it flattens out and widens:

Too high, and it lengthens and narrows:

Memory of what a runway should look like controls the mental process. There are some distortions. A long, narrow runway produces the impression that the aircraft is too high throughout the approach. A short, wide one has the opposite effect; but pilots learn to compensate for these variations.

The appearance of being high on approach in Concorde stems

from another visual trick. Because of the large angle of attack (13 degrees on final approach), the pitch angle is some 10 degrees above the horizon, compared with 2 to 3 degrees on most aircraft. As a result the runway, despite being the right shape, is simply lower down in the pilot's field of vision – he is looking down his nose at it. Although the picture of the runway is as it

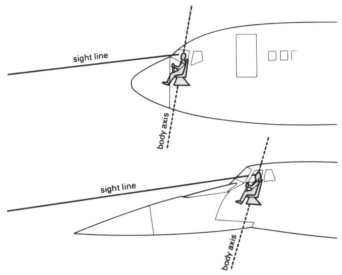

should be, it looks wrong – at least to start with. But the human mind is very adaptive and it does not take long before a corrective mechanism starts to work.

Apart from this odd visual feature, Concorde on the approach is very pleasant to fly. The good roll response, the light feel and the extraordinary stability make it easy to manoeuvre and give it a satisfying tendency to stay where it is put. The pilot concentrates on keeping it 'in the slot', flying with one hand while the other rests on the throttle levers, following the movements caused by the autothrottle system into which the required airspeed has been set.

Because the engines are below the body and wing, changes of power cause pitch-changes. Power increase: pitch up. Power decrease: pitch down. Most aircraft behave to some extent like this, so there is nothing wholly new to learn. Gusts are easy to deal with – the autothrottle almost sees them coming, and the autostab systems keep the aircraft on its flight path when other aircraft would wander off.

Final approach speed on a typical landing is 155 to 160 knots – about 180 mph. At a noise-sensitive airfield like Kennedy (or Heathrow), in reasonable weather conditions, the speed is kept at 190 knots (220 mph) until 800 feet altitude – about 2½ miles from the threshold. At the higher speed, less power is required to maintain the glideslope. In this case the speed is reduced, still under control of the autothrottle, between 800 and 500 feet. At 500 feet the speed is stable and the aircraft is about 1½ miles from the runway, lined up and ready to land.

'400 feet – a hundred to go.'

'300 feet – decision height.' (From this height a go-around would be started if the runway was not in view.)

'Continuing.'

The runway has been in sight all along, but the crew are behaving exactly as they would if the cloud base were low – a typical example of airline flying – taking the opportunity to practise for the case that really matters, when the situation isn't so good. On another day we might fly a fully automatic approach, as if for landing in fog. In that case, the decision height would be fifteen feet, and the procedure would be the same – only the numbers would change.

The Landing

'200 feet.'

The flight engineer, who cannot see the runway since he is behind and a little below the pilots, is reading the radio altimeters which are bouncing signals off the ground to determine height to within a foot.

'100 feet . . .

'50, 40, 30, 20, 15.'

At 40 feet the autothrottles are disconnected by pressing a small button on either side of the levers. A slight backward movement of the stick slows the rate of descent a little, pitching up perhaps a degree, from 10½ to 11½ degrees. The pilot's eye is still 75 feet above the runway (about the same height as a

747 pilot's) and he aims at a point about 2000 feet down the runway, knowing that the main wheels, trailing below and behind, will arrive well before that point.

From about 100-feet altitude we have been able to hear the 'ground effect' starting. A large wing, approaching the ground, begins at some point to squeeze the air between it and the surface, settling into a cushion of its own making. The large wing area and the high angle of attack make this effect more pronounced on Concorde than on conventional swept-wing aircraft, and seems to throw back some of the noise of air rushing into the engines. That is what it sounds like, at any rate.

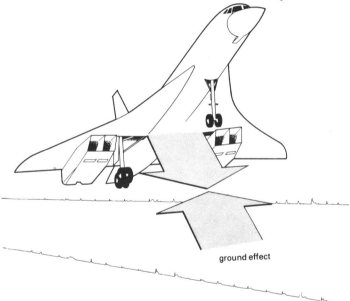

ground effect

At fifteen feet, the throttles are closed. The immediate effect is a tendency for the nose to drop. Landing is largely a matter of countering this tendency as the aeroplane settles into its ground effect. A slow backward movement of the stick keeps the nose where it is. The rate of movement depends on the strength of the pitch-down tendency. Good landings are simply a question of getting the balance right, so that the nose stays rock-steady against the far end of the runway.

Once on the ground there is a second landing to perform — the nosewheel is still a long way in the air. A nudge forward with the stick to get it on its way, followed by a backward movement to cushion its descent, and all the wheels have arrived.

As soon as the main wheels are on the ground, reverse thrust is engaged. Once the nosewheel is on, power is increased in reverse to kill the speed. At this point the stick is pushed fully forward to keep the nosewheel on the ground. With no lift from the now-level wings, the weight of the aircraft is borne on the wheels (principally the main ones) and the reverse thrust, acting above this new pivot point, tends to raise the nose.

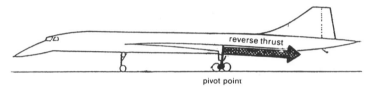

reverse thrust

pivot point

The elevons are still effective, though, and the nosewheel is kept firmly on the runway as braking starts. The powerful carbon discs get to work, the speed reduces, and the runway, which on touchdown didn't seem as long as it should be, with the eye still 35 feet in the air, lengthens again to its proper shape.

'100 knots.'

The two outboard throttles are pushed into reverse idle.

'75 knots.'

The inners follow.

'40 knots.'

All the engines are returned to forward idle power and the aeroplane is nearly ready to be turned off. It is easy, in any aeroplane, to think that the speed just after landing is lower than it really is, so a glance at the INS groundspeed is useful here.

Once we have turned off the runway, the nose is raised to the 5-degree position again, and the two inboard engines are shut down (at this weight, at the end of a flight, two engines provide quite enough power for taxying).

From runway 31 Left it is a longish taxi round to the British Airways terminal on the other side of the circle of airport buildings. As we approach it the time is a few minutes after 3.00 pm in London. Here, in New York, we are nearing our scheduled arrival time of 10.15 – apparently an hour before we left our gate at Heathrow. Just under four hours, gate to gate: an hour less than than it takes the earth to rotate through the angular distance separating London and New York. Three and a half hours' flight-time to cover three and a half thousand miles – an average speed of a thousand miles an hour.

Some of the disembarking passengers show signs of excitement – it has been their first supersonic flight, and it will be a while before they have sorted out the mixture of unreality and normality they have experienced. Others, the majority now, take it all for granted – they have probably used Concorde several times. And it has been normal. So it should be by now; but this normality had to be present from the first flight, in January 1976, and that took a little doing.

PART II
The Story

7. Building and Testing

Concorde's lineage goes back to the 1950s when the public, excited by the rapid advances in aviation caused by the jet engine, flocked to air shows to hear the supersonic booms made by fighters and research aircraft. The first supersonic level flight had been made by Chuck Yeager in October 1947 over the Mojave Desert. Rocket-propelled and launched from the air, the Bell X-1 demonstrated for the first time that there was no impenetrable aerodynamic wall at Mach 1, the speed of sound. Hair-raising though the flight and some of its successors were (and they quickly led to flight at Mach 2, the next year), they started an explosion of activity on both sides of the Atlantic and in the Soviet Union.

The British government had issued a specification for an experimental supersonic aircraft in 1943, and the vehicle was very nearly complete when the project was cancelled three years later. Britain instead adopted a programme of research using pilotless aircraft, which led in due course to its first operational Mach 2 fighter – the English Electric Lightning. Its prototype, the P1A, exceeded Mach 1 for the first time in August 1954. At about the same time the Fairey Delta 2 was exploring high-speed flight with its new wing shape, and on 10 March 1956 set a new world speed record of 1132 mph.

The Supersonic Race

In the same year the Supersonic Transport Advisory Committee (STAC) was set up in Britain to prepare for the first generation of supersonic passenger aircraft. It comprised representatives of all the major manufacturers of aircraft and engines, the airlines and various government departments, including the Royal Aircraft Establishment at Farnborough. Within two years the

STAC had concluded that a supersonic transport was feasible, seeing a future for two basic types: a Mach 1·2 medium-range airliner, and one which would cruise over 3500 miles at about Mach 1·8. The faster, longer-range version was preferred – it seemed to offer a real advantage in speed over the subsonic jets which were already flying. Of all the wing shapes studied, the refined delta, suitable for speeds around Mach 2 and above, was the most promising.

But there was another choice to be made. Studies indicated that between Mach 2 and Mach 3 there was a slight improvement in overall cruise efficiency, so it might pay to take an even bigger step forward. However, although by now there was a good deal of experience of flight at Mach 2, there was none at all at Mach 3. Furthermore, it was known that at speeds much above Mach 2 friction heating of the skin would go above the limits for conventional aluminium alloys, and new materials, principally steel and titanium, would be needed. These are much more difficult to work, and the industry had little knowledge of their use. Finally, it seemed that the advantages for the passenger in reducing total flight times (which include taxying, take-off and landing) were enormous at Mach 2, but much less evident at higher speeds.

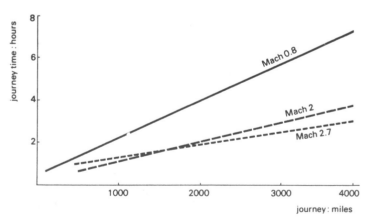

Comparative journey times

By the end of the 1950s the British direction had become clear, and two experimental aircraft were built in order to study the qualities of the delta wing. The Handley-Page HP115 first

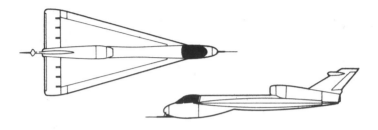

Handley-Page HP115

flew in 1961. Essentially a heavily swept-back delta wing with a cockpit and engine attached as if by afterthought, this aircraft was used exclusively to explore the low-speed qualities of the wing – in particular its known propensity to produce vortex lift.

Its companion, the BAC Type 221, was a rebuild of the Fairey Delta 2, with the wing now refined to a double-curved 'ogee' shape. This wing, already known to have advantages over

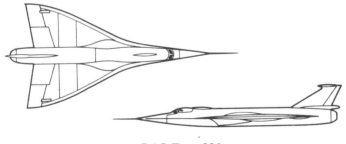

BAC Type 221

the simple delta, was a direct precursor of Concorde's. The aircraft first flew in 1964, and was used to study both the low- and high-speed qualities of the wing.

The information gained from these two aircraft led to contracts being placed by the government to research a Mach 2 airliner. The first attempt, known as the Bristol Type 198, was to have been a six-engined delta aircraft. But early studies showed that the six-engined configuration was a mistake. The centre engine of the group of three under each wing would, when shut down, produce interference with the air entering the other two. The aircraft also showed signs of being too heavy. It was followed, in 1961, with a proposal for an aircraft designated the BAC Type 223. (Bristol Aircraft had by now been absorbed into the new British Aircraft Corporation.) It was to have four Olympus engines – already in service with the Vulcan bomber – a delta wing and a 'droop' nose.

At the Paris Air Show of 1961 the French Sud-Aviation company unveiled plans for their 'Super-Caravelle' – a supersonic airliner whose size and shape were very similar to the 223's. The French aircraft industry had been devastated by the Second World War but was now in a period of vigorous revival. In 1954, the year in which Britain's P1A had gone supersonic, a French aircraft, the delta-winged Gerfault 1A, had done the same. There followed a line of research and military aircraft,

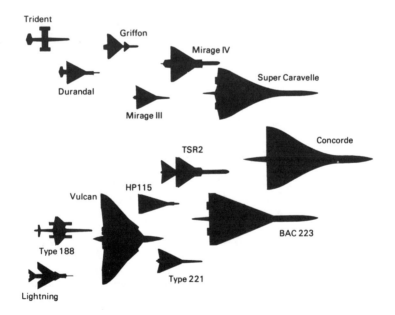

most notably the Mirage and Mystère series, which firmly established France in the small group of nations with experience of Mach 2 flying. The Super-Caravelle showed one major difference from the British design, however: it was designed for medium-range. The subsonic Caravelle had been the only European commercial success in the jet-airliner market. It was a medium-range aircraft, and Sud-Aviation saw their new design as a natural successor.

There were, then, two converging lines of development, one on each side of the Channel, both leading directly towards a huge leap into commercial supersonics.

In engineering and design terms, there was every reason to merge the two schemes, but politics provided the necessary catalyst. Britain at the time was negotiating to enter the Common Market, and saw General de Gaulle, with his deep suspicions of Britain's Atlantic connection, as its principal obstacle. A major industrial venture of this kind, with its implication of long-term cooperation against the major aeronautical competition, the USA, seemed an attractive dowry, an alliance which would improve the prospects of entry to Europe. France's political interests in the project were different, though it certainly shared the view that competition with the USA, which held 85 per cent of the commercial aviation market, would require intra-European cooperation. There were other reasons: British technology had something to offer, the only available engine was the Bristol-Siddeley Olympus and, perhaps more importantly, the price of building and testing such an aircraft was likely to be so great that cost-sharing by the two countries was the only possible way to tackle it.

The agreement between the two governments was signed on 29 November 1962. They were to share the costs of development and production, and the revenues from sales. The two most remarkable features of the agreement were that the companies concerned were to set up a joint management structure for the project and that there was no break-clause. The first ensured that enormous numbers of British and French people would work with each other and for each other for many years, and the second made sure that neither government could back out without the agreement of its partner.

In the United States, progress had been rapid, spurred by the

Korean war. The first of the Century series of supersonic fighters, the F100 Super Sabre, was in squadron service by 1955. The next year saw the large, delta-winged B-58 Hustler in the air. The North American B-70 Mach 3 bomber was being designed, in steel and titanium. It looked as if the classic American system of development was about to happen again: as if, like the B-47 bomber which had paved the way for the whole generation of civil subsonic transports, the B-70 would, at a cost only to the military, provide the expertise necessary to design an advanced supersonic transport. But the cost was too great. In 1959 the development of the B-70 was stopped. Two aircraft remained – memorials to the supplanting of the manned bomber by the missile.

This abrupt end to the supersonic bomber programme influenced the whole of the development of its civil counterpart. It meant that all costs would be attributable to the project itself. It was already known that these would be extremely high, too high for private risk capital, and the American taxpayer would be asked to bear the burden directly – to subsidize. To the public, if it considered the question at all, it seemed only just that its expenditures on defence should carry a return in the form of an extremely successful aircraft manufacturing industry, but direct funding of a civil project proved to be a highly sensitive political issue.

Then, in 1960, President Kennedy came to power and the atmosphere changed. The success of the Soviet space programme had dealt shattering blows to American self-esteem, and this was a time for the restoration of confidence. Challenges had to be taken up, and the growing competition from Europe and the USSR was seen in that light. A committee under Najeeb Halaby, the administrator of the Federal Aviation Agency, was set up 'to develop the safest, most efficient and most economical aviation system attainable'. It was still studying the difficult problem of how to catch up with the Europeans, who by now had gone into joint action, when in June 1963 Juan Trippe, the president of Pan American, took out options on six Concordes. This move galvanized the system into action. President Kennedy announced that 'the country should be prepared to invest the funds and the effort necessary to maintain the national lead in long-range aircraft – a lead we have held since the Second

World War, a lead we should make every responsible effort to maintain'. The competition for the US SST had started.

In the Soviet Union, too, the 1950s had seen enormous advances. The MIG series, in particular the MIG21, had become increasingly impressive combat vehicles. In civil terms (although the distinction between civil and military aircraft was not always clear) they had followed behind, producing aircraft of similar pattern to those built in the West, usually a little cruder, heavier and with less attractive interiors. Work is believed to have started on the Soviet supersonic transport soon after the Anglo-French agreement was signed in 1962. A British delegation led by Julian Amery MP was shown a model of the aircraft during a visit to Moscow in 1963. It looked remarkably like Concorde. Suspicions of espionage, which started then, were reinforced when in 1967 two Czechoslovakian priests were arrested in Toulouse. After a trial at which evidence was given of microfilm smuggled in toothpaste tubes found in the first-class lavatory of the Ostend–Warsaw Express, they were given heavy sentences.

Concorde's manufacturers have never believed the espionage theory, but whether or not it be true it is clear that the Soviet designers, led by Alexei Tupolev, settled early on for the Mach 2, alloy-structure, delta-winged type of aircraft. Given this, there was every reason why the two aircraft should look alike. There were, however, some very important differences: Tupolev's wing was of a simpler shape, and the engines, which were turbofans, were grouped together in one pod below the fuselage.

There were thus, in 1963, three groups in the race for supersonic transports. The Anglo-French (or Franco-British, depending on which side of the Channel you lived) team was at work. Sales options had been taken out by Pan American, closely followed by BOAC and Air France. At the same time, suspicions were beginning to build that the cost of the project was not under control. The Labour Party, which had not objected to the treaty the previous year, began to be critical. Environmental opposition started, with the publication in the *Observer* of a series of articles pointing out the potential dangers of supersonic flight, in particular of the boom.

In the United States, Boeing, Lockheed and North American were working on design studies for a Mach 3 aircraft – Mach 3 because it had been decided to enter the race with a superior vehicle; one which, although it might appear a little later, would have clear advantages over the competition because of its greater capacity and range. In the USSR, work had started on the TU144 in complete secrecy and, it turned out later, at great speed.

Building and Testing

The early years of the Concorde project were devoted largely to testing – materials, variations of the wing shape, structures – and to refining the design. In May 1964 came the final resolution of the overlapping concepts of the British and French teams, a proposal for an aircraft carrying up to 118 passengers on intercontinental journeys. It met with approval and the design was 'frozen' at this point for the prototypes. There were to be two more major design changes later, but at last the time had come to stop talking and start building. In April 1965 metal was cut for the prototypes.

Four airframes were built initially – two prototypes and two structural test specimens. These latter were installed in rigs in huge laboratories, one in Toulouse and the other at Farnborough. Each rig could heat and cool the structure to extreme temperatures, while hydraulic jacks tortured it with stresses up to and beyond those for which it was designed. The rig in France examined the strength of the wing and fuselage. It imposed static loads, and, towards the end of the programme, deliberately broke parts of the structure. At Farnborough an even more elaborate installation enclosed the body and wing in a jacket through which hot or cold air was blown, enabling it to simulate real flights in about one third of the time. It was designed to examine the fatigue strength of the whole structure. By the end of 1974 it had completed 6800 cycles, and from then on continued to produce about 7000 simulated flights per year – staying well ahead of the real aircraft.

These two models comprised in themselves the most thorough and advanced structural programme in the history of aviation. They were backed up by many other rigs: smaller sections of the aircraft were also tested at the two centres, and so were the windows and windshields – by, among other methods, firing dead chickens at them. The fuel system rig was also a monstrous affair, which reared up to simulate accelerations – to slosh the fuel around in the tanks, and make the pumps work uphill. There were full-scale models of the electrical and airconditioning systems which, like all the others, were subjected to extreme temperature changes. The hydraulics rig in a hangar at Blagnac airport, Toulouse, included the full flying control system and the undercarriage mechanism. It was attached to the design simulator which was housed in the same building so that it could be controlled from an actual flight deck.

This simulator, commissioned in 1966, was used extensively during the design of the aircraft – perhaps the first time flight simulation had entered so completely into this area. Programmed, as it were, straight from the drawing-board, defined by equations worked out by the aerodynamicists, it was used to study Concorde's flight characteristics – the behaviour of a new type of aircraft which had not yet flown. The science of aerodynamics has, at any rate in most pilots' opinion, always included a fair degree of plain, old-fashioned guesswork, so it must have required considerable faith to make refinements to the design on this basis. But it worked. The design simulator in fact produced a reasonably faithful representation of the aircraft's behaviour, although it was rather harder to fly than the real thing. In addition to its role in the design, the simulator was used to prepare the crews for the first flights. It was also linked to the French air traffic control system, to study Concorde's interaction with the day-to-day pattern of flights.

Production of the prototypes and of all subsequent models was split equally between the two countries. Factories all over Europe and the USA produced components which were shipped to Toulouse or Filton to be put together into complete subassemblies.

Each centre of production specialized in certain sections: the wing and centre-fuselage were made at Toulouse, the nose and tail in Filton; the engines in England, the intakes in France. Once completed, each sub-assembly was either used on the factory's own production line or shipped across the Channel to the other one, usually in the cavernous interior of a 'Super Guppy' freighter. Each of the two factories assembled alternate aircraft in the production run.

		Manufacturer
01	Fuselage nose	BAC Filton
02	Droop nose	Marshalls
03	Forward fuselage	BAC Filton
04	Rear fuselage	BAC Weybridge
05	Fin	BAC Weybridge
06	Rudder	BAC Weybridge
	Nacelles comprising:	
07	Air intake	BAC Filton
08	Engine bay	BAC Filton
09	Nozzles	SNECMA
—	Engines	Rolls-Royce – Bristol
10	Intermediate fuselage	BAC Filton
11	Centre wing	SUD Toulouse + H. Dubois
12	Forward wing	SUD Suresnes
13	Centre wing	SUD Suresnes + La Courneuve
14	Centre wing	SUD Toulouse
15	Centre wing	SUD Toulouse
16	Elevons	SUD Suresnes
17	Centre wing	SUD Toulouse + Fiat
18	Outer wing	AMD Dassault
19	Landing gear main	Hispano Suiza
20	Landing gear nose	Messier

Filton

Toulouse

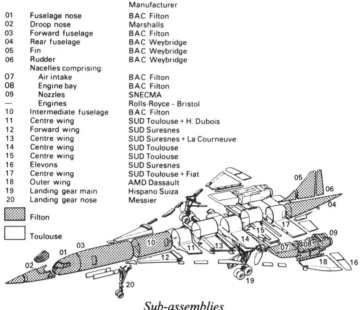

Sub-assemblies

This division of labour, which existed through all aspects of design, testing and manufacture, involved a spectacular exercise in logistics. It also meant that each team worked with both metric and imperial measurements. I remember seeing, much later, two sub-assemblies of one of the production aircraft being joined together. One section had been made in France and the other in Britain. Both were given time to get to the same temperature. Even the rivets which were used to join them were heated to the exact degree. The fit was perfect.

In fact, the whole of Concorde's building was full of marvellous engineering. Pictures can only give an impression of the precision with which each piece was fitted on, of the careful way each aircraft grew, of the pride the builders took in its assembly. I was lucky enough to see the 747 being built, too. That project, itself in terms of size and speed one of the great feats of modern industry, gave the impression of aircraft techniques applied on shipbuilding scales. The scale of Concorde's building was quite different – more like watchmaking carried out in a hangar.

Structural testing, simulator proving and manufacture continued. The first prototype, the French-built 001, was rolled out in December 1967. By August 1968 it was carrying out taxi trials. A month later its fellow, 002, was completed at Filton. In December the ground-testing of the Olympus 593 engine had reached the 5000-hour point. Well over a hundred hours of flight testing had also taken place with an engine attached to the underside of a Vulcan bomber. The first flight was getting very close. And the TU144 flew – on the last day of 1968.

It is impossible to know how developed the TU144 was by the time of its first flight. The blanket of secrecy had been lifted only to show it in construction to a British delegation earlier in the year, and it had appeared to have a long way to go then. Its first flight was also the first time its four Kusnetsov engines, specially developed for the aircraft, had been in the air. It is likely, however, that the rush to get airborne extracted a heavy penalty later.

001's preparation for its first flight took place, by contrast, in the glare of international publicity. Originally scheduled for February 1968, the flight had been put back several times. The taxi trials in August revealed brake problems which called for extensive modifications. The Western world's press had followed these tribulations with increasing interest – they fitted into the pattern of increasing costs and the growing concern expressed by some writers about the safety of supersonic flight. On 2 March 1969, after two days of mist which introduced a final delay, 001 took off from Toulouse.

André Turcat piloted the aircraft on a 42-minute flight, taking it up to an indicated airspeed of 250 knots at 10,000 feet. Not surprisingly, the objectives of this first flight were limited to assessment of the controls and calibration of the airspeed indicators with that of the 'chase' aircraft, but it was wholly successful – the machine handled even better than the design simulator had led the pilots to expect.

Turcat, who is now retired from flying, was a most unusual test pilot. Academically distinguished and singularly purposeful, he was marked for success early in his career. He had been the chief pilot of Nord and had flown at Mach 2 as early as 1959 in its Griffon fighter. As Director of Flight Test (an appointment made directly by the French government), he was certainly one of the driving forces behind the Concorde project. His single-mindedness and sense of conviction sometimes seemed like arrogance, but he could be charming, too. There has never been any doubt about his skills as a test pilot or an administrator. The rest of the crew on 001's first flight were Jacques Guignard, the co-pilot, who retired soon after for reasons of health; Jacques Retif, the flight engineer; Henri Perrier, the chief observer, who was later to become Turcat's successor as Director of Flight Test; Claude Durand, flight test observer; and Jean Belon, Assistant Chief of Flight Test for SNECMA, the French engine manufacturer.

001 made a further eight flights before 002 took off from Filton on 9 April. Brian Trubshaw was in command. The flight was not without its problems. First, the captain's airspeed indicator had been persistently misbehaving during the runway trials. On each, the warning flag had come into view at 90 knots, indicating that the information was unreliable, although the needle which showed the speed appeared to agree with the co-pilot's instrument. After several attempts, the engineers felt they had cured the problem, but no one could be quite sure. If the flag came down again on the day, the take-off would have to be aborted. In fact, it did not, and the take-off was without further difficulties. But then a further electronic neurosis struck – both radio altimeters failed. That would make the landing difficult.

At this stage, and for some while into the test programme, landings were being made in a simplified way – little was known about the exact technique which would be needed to combat the tendency for the nose to drop when the aircraft entered the ground effect. So the power was kept on until touchdown, to remove at least part of the difficulty. In addition, height judgment was difficult from the pilot's position 35 feet above the wheels. Radio altimeters showing the precise distance between the wheels and the runway were invaluable for this purpose. During the flight the observers tried to restore the instruments, while the crew had yet another problem to deal with – a light aircraft had wandered into their path and the radar controller, unable to contact it, was giving 'steers' to Concorde in order to keep it away from this danger. The light aircraft finally moved away, but the radio altimeters stayed out of action. So Trubshaw's first landing, on his aircraft's first flight, was done purely by eye – plain, old-fashioned pilot's eyeball. The whole flight, from Filton to Fairford, whose longer runway would be used for all subsequent tests, took just 42 minutes – strangely enough, exactly the same time as 001's maiden flight.

Brian Trubshaw had been with Vickers for seventeen years before they were absorbed into BAC. He flew in the test programmes of the Viscount, the Vanguard, the Valiant bomber, the VC10 and the BAC 111. He had prepared himself for Mach 2, delta-winged flight with sorties in Vulcans, Mirages and Lightnings. He also flew the American B-58 Hustler. All this was very necessary, but his background in the testing of airliners was perhaps his most important contribution to Concorde. Of all the pilots in the test groups, he had most knowledge of how airline people thought, and so he was often able to influence the project in sensible, practical ways.

The co-pilot on this flight was John Cochrane, a lively Scotsman who had come to the programme from the RAF, through the testing of the Vickers VC10. Brian Watts, BAC's chief flight engineer, was in the third seat. The flight test observers, who monitored the vast array of recording devices in the cabin, were John Allan, Peter Holding (who later joined the programme as a flight engineer) and Michael Addley.

The details of the first few flights make interesting reading, presented baldly as they were in the first issue of the internally produced *Concorde Flight News*, dated 23 June 1969.

Flight Details

Date	Aircraft and flight number	Flight time (hrs, mins.)	
2 March 1969	001/1	0·42	First flight
			Pilot's assessment
			Altitude to 10,000 feet
			Airspeed to 250 knots
			Speed comparison with chase aircraft
			Brake parachute

Date	Aircraft and flight number	Flight time (hrs, mins.)	
8 March	001/2	1·17	Altitude to 15,000 feet Airspeed to 300 knots Landing gear retraction and extension at 220 knots Droop nose functioned between 12° and 5° Simulated missed approach Trim curve determination Air brake operation Assessment with and without artificial feel Simulated 3-engine approach Landing measurement
13 March	001/3	1·12	Simulated engine cut on take-off Assessment without auto-stabilization Standby lowering of undercarriage Cruise performance Fuel jettison system testing
17 March	001/4	1·20	Altitude to 20,000 feet Airspeed to 330 knots, Mach 0·66 Assessment of approach configuration with flying controls on mechanical mode Engine No. 1 shut down and re-lit Landing with auto-stabilization off Nacelle cooling secondary flap investigation

Date	Aircraft and flight number	Flight time (hrs, mins.)	
21 March	001/5	1·33	Airspeed 350 knots Performance checks at 15,000 feet, 300 knots Engines 2, 3 and 4 shut down and relit at 15,000 feet, 250 knots
28 March	001/6	1·38	Altitude to 26,000 feet Airspeed to Mach 0·75 Landing with nose in 5° position
30 March	001/7	1·25	Measurement of rate of climb with simulated failure of No. 4 engine Position error measurement Study of descent configuration at 300 knots Study of lateral handling in the landing configuration
30 March	001/8	1·16	First in-flight switch-on of after-burning
2 April	001/9	1·41	Altitude to 30,000 feet Airspeed to 350 knots, Mach 0·80 Afterburner light up at 20,000 feet 2G0 and 350 knots Approach and landing without autothrottle and without ILS GTS [gas turbine starters] investigation

Date	Aircraft and flight number	Flight time (hrs, mins.)	
9 April	002/1	0·42	First flight of aircraft 002 Pilot's assessment Altitude to 8000 feet Airspeed to 280 knots Speed comparison with chase aircraft Brake parachute Take-off measurement
16 April	002/2	1·12	Altitude to 9000 feet Nose raised to 5°

28 April	002/3	1·04	Altitude to 15,000 feet
			Airspeed to 350 knots
			Landing gear retraction
			   and extension
			Assessment without auto-
			   stabilization
			Trim curve determination
			Air brake operation
			Simulated engine cut on
			   take-off
			Roll power
			Fuel jettison system testing

8 May	002/4	1·22	Altitude to 25,000 feet
			Airspeed to 350 knots
			Handling checks
			Climb performance checks
			Fuel feed checks
			Nose free fall 5–12°
			Drag check with under-
			   carriage down
			Simulated 3-engine
			   go-around

Date	Aircraft and flight number	Flight time (hrs, mins.)	
13 May	002/5	1·30	Continuation of flying qualities investigation commenced in flight 002/4 Relights of all four engines at 15,000 feet and 250 knots Stand-by lowering of undercarriage Simulated 3-engine approach Simulated 2-engine approach

And so on. This list, of course, gives no idea of the amount of preparation that went into each flight, the long debriefing afterwards, the examination of recorder traces, the analysis of results. But it does show the patient, steady exploration of the flight envelope and the deliberate entry into failure cases, even from quite early on in the proceedings. At this stage in any airliner's testing, one must remember, the crew have to be able to bale out. Happily, it was never necessary.

By 10 July the flight envelope had been extended to 40,000 feet, an indicated airspeed of 380 knots and a Mach number of 0·8. The aircraft had taken off at a weight of 133 tons and had flown at a minimum speed of 138 knots and an angle of attack of 16·5 degrees. The total flight time to date was 62 hours 18 minutes. Forced excitation (flutter) tests started. These in-flight experiments, a most important part of flight test work, examine the structural damping of the aircraft. Control surfaces are made to move suddenly and then released. The object is to see how long it takes for the resulting oscillations to die out, and to what extent they are transmitted to the aeroplane's structure – to ensure, in fact, that the tail does not wag the dog. The initial motion can be induced by 'bonkers' (small rocket packs attached to the control surfaces), by an out-of-balance motor working on the flight control hydraulics, or by simply jerking the stick. In addition to these methods, Concorde used an electronic stick-jerk box which could apply precisely controlled inputs to the flying controls.

The aircraft were then grounded for the fitting of their new variable intakes, which were needed for flight above Mach 1. In October, 001 went supersonic for the first time. This was followed by the first airline assessment of the aeroplane's flying qualities. Captains Paul Roitsch of Pan American, Maurice Bernard of Air France, Vernon Laursen of TWA and James Andrew of BOAC each flew 001 for about two hours. Their flights included a cruise at Mach 1·2 at 43,000 feet, a wide selection of simulated failures (at their choice) and approaches in various configurations. Jimmy Andrew ended with a landing in a crosswind of 22 knots – the highest encountered at that stage. With the reservation that they had not yet been to the full cruise speed and height, they agreed on their general impressions:

> For all the flight conditions flown during this first phase, the aircraft was pleasant and easy to fly, imposed no excessive workload on the pilot, even in failure conditions, and there should be no problems in training airline pilots and engineers to handle the aircraft.

The year 1970 saw a continuous extension of the flight envelope into the areas where the production aircraft would be spending most of their lives. It was a successful, productive year for the prototypes. Both aircraft reached Mach 2 for the first time, at a height of 52,000 feet.

From Mach 1·5 upwards, the programme entered the 'high risk' phase, an area where no aircraft of this size, civil or military, had ever been. A long, straight route was required for these tests so that plenty of time could be spent at high speeds. It needed also to be within good radar coverage, to be close to emergency airfields and to be in reach of rescue services.

Set up primarily for this purpose, 'Boom Alley', as it became known, was also used to measure, objectively and subjectively, the effects of the boom. It is doubtful whether the measurements

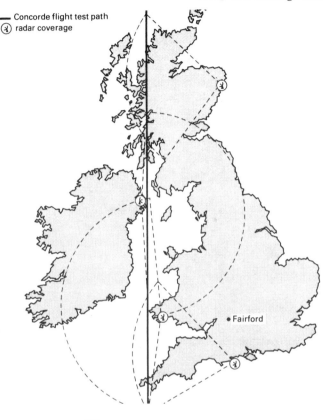

Concorde flight test path
(ч) radar coverage

• Fairford

The western test route

were well enough planned to contribute much to the existing knowledge of sonic boom effects, and the report was never published, but the trials certainly had an effect on the public. Stories of broken windows and frightened children made good reading, and the enormous press interest gave the anti-Concorde lobby its biggest boost so far. The public response to the trials had some curious features. An enterprising Scottish couple claimed that what they described as their 'rhythm' method of contraception had been interrupted; and large numbers of complaints came in on days when, although previously advertised, no flight took place. There is no doubt, though, that some people were genuinely alarmed. The series of tests brought to an end whatever hopes the manufacturers may still have entertained of supersonic flight over Britain.

In the aircraft, despite accusations that they were deliberately steering off course to confuse the boom measurements, the crews were, in fact, carrying out flutter tests, slam acceleration of the engines, sideslips, pushovers (to induce negative 'g' forces), single and double engine cuts. During the development of the B-58, two aircraft had been lost while performing engine cuts at Mach 2. Concorde could not afford any losses – the project would almost certainly be cancelled if that were to happen – so progress through the régime was careful, prudent. Each step was examined in the simulator beforehand. No breakthroughs were looked for, just gradual, empiric testing and observation.

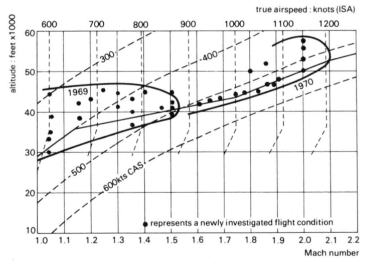

As the tests progressed, confidence in the aircraft's ability to cope with the effects of failures at high Mach numbers grew. Most of the failures were deliberately induced, but in January 1971 an intake ramp became detached when the afterburner was shut down at Mach 1·98. Pieces of metal were ingested by the engine, which continued to 'windmill' although seriously damaged. The aircraft landed, perfectly safely, using its remaining three engines, and the incident – unpleasant as it was – provided welcome evidence that the immensely strong wall between each engine and its neighbour would contain such damage, as it was designed to do.

Concorde started to show her paces. President Pompidou went up in 001 for the first time in May 1971, and again later in the year to meet President Nixon in the Azores. The first intercontinental flight was logged – 2500 miles to Dakar in Senegal. Model 01, the first pre-production aircraft, was completed in Filton and flown for the first time. By the middle of 1972, over 1000 hours had been logged by the three aeroplanes, and the first sales tour took place – a 45,000-mile demonstration run around twelve countries in the Middle and Far East and Australia. The tour was flown by Brian Trubshaw in 002, whose older-model engines had not been fitted with the improved combustion chambers which were designed to cut out the trails of smoke left behind on take-off and landing. Perhaps this was an unfortunate choice, for the magnificent feat of time-keeping and logistics was somewhat marred by 'Smoky Joe's' anti-social habits.

On the tour, two features of the aircraft which were later to cause problems began to announce themselves. The take-off from Athens was rough. The runway was known to have undulations in it, but Concorde's long, narrow fuselage amplified the shocks coming up through the main wheels so that quite unpleasant 'g' forces built up on the crew just at the moment of rotation for take-off. At this stage the forces were manageable, but what about heavier take-off weights, other runways? Later, Trubshaw and Turcat revisited Athens to investigate the runway roughness effect. Their judgments about its acceptability to airlines differed. There would be further trials.

On departure from Tehran the same day, at light weight and climbing into very cold air, it turned out to be difficult to keep the Mach number within bounds when temperature changes were encountered. The autopilot tended to 'chase' the Mach number. Control was made no easier by the fact that 002's intakes, still at a comparatively early stage of development, required restricted use of the throttles. The improvements already in the pipeline seemed likely to solve this problem, but a real solution was found only just before entry into service.

In July 1972 BOAC and Air France signed contracts for delivery of aircraft in 1975: five for BOAC and four for Air France. The relationship between the manufacturers and the airlines suddenly became very real, and the test programme entered its final phase. There were other visits abroad for demonstration purposes, notably by 02 to Dallas,Texas, for the opening of the new Dallas–Fort Worth Airport, to Rio de Janeiro, Brazil, and, in 1974, to the west coast of the USA, to Peru, Colombia and Venezuela. There was also a spectacular demonstration of speed. 02 flew from Boston to Paris and back, completing the round trip while a scheduled Air France 747 was *en route* from Paris to Boston. In parallel with these flights, 002 went to Johannesburg for performance trials at a 'hot and high' field (Jan Smuts Airport is nearly 6000 feet above sea level), and for similar tests to Torrejon, near Madrid. 02 flew to Fairbanks, Alaska, for 'cold soak' tests.

In the last month of 1973 the first production aircraft, 201, took off on its maiden flight from Toulouse. The fact that it reached Mach 1·57 on its first flight demonstrated that flight testing of Concorde was now a mature art. The aircraft had grown through three models: prototype, pre-production and production. Two of each of the first two types had been built, and there was now authorization for a total of sixteen production aircraft.

The pre-production models were longer than the prototypes: the fuselage in front of the wings was extended to accommodate more seats. Both also had the new, fully glazed visor to improve visibility for the pilots.

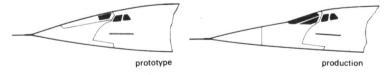

prototype   production

The wings were more refined, too. The leading edges had been redesigned, and twist and camber added to the outer sections. The engines had increased in power. For the production aircraft, two other features were incorporated: an extended tail-cone (also fitted to 02), for reduced drag at Mach 2, and the new thrust reverser/nozzle units at the rear of the engines. The aircraft now had room for up to 128 passengers and their baggage, and was capable of carrying them on trans-Atlantic routes.

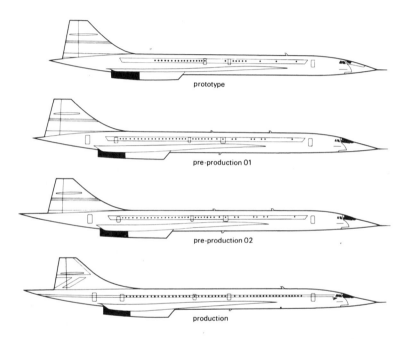

prototype

pre-production 01

pre-production 02

production

In August 1974 the second production aircraft, 202, went to the Arabian Gulf states and then on to Singapore to test the runway response. On the way to Singapore, operating as guest co-pilot, I saw for myself the intrusions of warmer air into the stratosphere – nothing alarming, but they required some attention from the pilot to smooth them out. It was a wonderful ride, though, with marvellous views of India and Sumatra, and the aircraft working beautifully. We ran down the Straits of Malacca, descending into Singapore at the end of what felt like an almost disappointingly short flight.

The trials demonstrated to everyone's satisfaction that at heavy weights, on some runways (and Singapore's was in poor shape, though it was later put right), the oscillations were not acceptable for airline service. Either the runway had to be reasonably free from undulations or the aircraft weight had to be kept down. It was a situation we could live with temporarily, for all the main airfields we would be using to start with had perfectly suitable runways, but it was obvious that it was not tolerable in the long run. The trials had, however, provided the information necessary to begin the design of an undercarriage modification which would damp out the bumps.

During the stay in Singapore I began to get to know Brian Trubshaw. He does not conform much to the standard image of a test pilot. Stocky, and of medium height, he appeared at first sight rather fierce – perhaps a little wary – but he laughs easily, and when he does his face cracks wide open, revealing his warmth. If it's a particularly good joke, the laugh turns into a guffaw, and the shoulders shake.

At a pre-flight briefing he is intense, and listens carefully. Flying, he hunches a little over the controls, taking a firm grip on the aeroplane. I sat behind him on many of the take-offs from the rough runway. They were far from comfortable. What was so impressive was that each discovery of a bump in the runway was followed by another trial which deliberately sought out the same bump, at perhaps a higher weight or speed. Trubshaw went patiently through the whole series, until the evidence was complete.

The experiments over, we returned to Bahrain then flew the aircraft back to Fairford. In the right-hand seat again on this last leg, I was ideally placed to see what I am sure is a unique piece of time-warping. We left Bahrain minutes after sunrise. Flying at Mach 2 westwards towards the Mediterranean we left the sun behind. When we were somewhere between Cyprus and Crete it set behind us. We then turned north-west, to fly up past Greece. This effectively reduced our westerly speed and the sun began to come up for the second time. As it popped up above the eastern horizon we started to descend. Our descent rate then outpaced the sun's rise, and it set once more. Finally, as we flew subsonically across northern Italy, it caught up with us again. After that, the third sunrise in two hours, it stayed up.

Certification trials continued in Casablanca, where take-off and landing noise was measured. At Moses Lake, in Washington State, John Cochrane sought natural icing to validate earlier trials in England which had been carried out by pouring water into freezing air in front of Concorde from a Canberra tanker. A final visit was made to Madrid where take-off, landing and climb performance were measured.

All these trials were part of the programme laid down by the joint airworthiness authorities of Britain and France. Certification requirements were set out in the TSS (Transport Supersonique) standards. This vast document defined in precise detail how a supersonic airliner would be judged in order to receive its Certificate of Airworthiness. It imposed standards of performance, of structural strength, of stability, of system design, of handling qualities, which in many ways were more severe than any previous ones. It was against this background that the enormous test programme – more than 5000 hours in total – was carried out.

There was just one more part to come: route-proving, in which the airlines were expected to play a major part.

8. The Nucleus Group

Just where and when we would begin scheduled services was far from clear at the beginning of 1975, but the first aircraft was due to be delivered towards the end of the year and it seemed far from certain that permission to enter the USA, Concorde's prime market, would be obtained by then. Alternatives were needed. Air France's plans clarified first – they would go via Dakar to Rio de Janeiro. The French government was able to clear this potentially profitable route quickly. Our best choice was Bahrain, which, although it did not in itself provide a large enough market to sustain a service, was the first stop on a planned route to Singapore and Australia.

Despite the uncertainties, work had to start early in the year in order to get ready for what would clearly be the most public and closely scrutinized inaugural flight in the history of civil aviation. Of course, we were also preparing for all the regular flights that would follow. Meanwhile, the test programme required that, as the final stage before certification, the aeroplane should be flown by airline crews over typical routes, and that it should be maintained by airline engineers.

Training began in March. Eight captains and eight flight engineers reported to Filton for the start of the ground school. This first course was a test of character as well as ability. The instructors were a devoted and hard-working group, but they had a lot to contend with. Although most of the system models were working, and the lectures were well-prepared, the manuals were something of a mess – partly because they had been written by a committee using a standard and somewhat limited vocabulary which could be adapted to both French and English. Printed from a computer which stored all the agreed procedures, the format was shatteringly repetitive – almost unreadable. The fact that each paragraph finished with '/END/' seemed to add a touch of mania to the soul-less text. Much of it had to be rewritten later. Another, very real difficulty arose from the fact that the aircraft was still changing. The test programme was still going on, and modifications were being incorporated. Occasionally an instructor would be interrupted in the middle of the description of some complicated circuit with news that it had been replaced. He needed to be able to think on his feet.

Some degree of confusion is only to be expected on a first course. We all accepted it willingly as part of the price to be paid for being members of the nucleus group, and at least it added interest. Sitting the first examination was another part of the price – some of the questions showed that the examiners were learning, too. The sight of sixteen middle-aged men opening the test papers, whose contents were so crucial to their careers, hovered somewhere between hilarity and tragedy. Suppressed curses at a turgidly worded question, murmurs of appreciation when an answer was easily recognized – these were followed by a repertoire of head-scratching, pencil-chewing and leg-changing that any other, much younger student would recognize. The gathering afterwards to compare notes would be familiar, too.

An employee of BAC, who had sat through the course with us simply to see how well it worked, adopted a novel approach: whenever one of the multi-choice questions baffled him he simply chose the longest answer, reasoning that the examiners would have given most thought to the correct one. He passed. None of us were as clever as that – we simply battled through. An analysis afterwards showed his line of thought to be uncomfortably right, so the answers were re-worded for future courses. I doubt if this is a useful technique for passing more settled examinations, but it was pleasant to think that there must have been almost as much pencil-chewing up at the CAA as there had been in our classroom.

We left Filton in a spring blizzard for the next stage – in Toulouse. The design simulator (the only one in existence at the time) had been refurbished to the standard of the production aircraft, so we were able to use it for our training by the manufacturer's crews. Staying in a hotel close enough to allow us to walk to the hangar in the mornings, we relaxed in the town after work. Toulouse, like Bristol, has been associated with the aircraft business for many years. It is a mixture of industrial modernity and narrow, winding streets. In one of the narrowest is La Corde, an ancient restaurant of no great pretensions, whose excellent *terrine de campagne* and *cassoulet* became our staple diet. Large quantities of Corbière, a local red wine, fuelled our interminable discussions of the day's flying. Bits of news broke in from the outside world. Battle had been joined by Concorde's opponents – several of them British – at the public hearings on the recently published US Environmental Impact Statement.

In June we started flying at Fairford, in Gloucestershire, from where all the British test work had been done. It was a glorious month, one of those English Junes which light up the country-side and restore one's memory of what summer should be like. G-BBDG, the first production aircraft out of Filton, dressed fully in British Airways livery, was there for our use. The simulator course had been somewhat shorter than that performed by later groups, so our aircraft time included supersonic flying. During the two weeks it took to complete the nine flying details, we each logged about twenty hours, including Mach 2 flights around the Bay of Biscay.

While we were completing our training, Air France began their share of the route-proving. Over a period of nine weeks they made 125 flights covering 368,000 miles in 375 hours of block time. Their journeys from Paris covered Dakar, Rio de Janeiro, Lisbon, Caracas, Gander, Keflavik in Iceland and Bodo in Norway, Shannon, Tangier, Lyon, Marseilles, Lille and Nice. All the flights carried invited passengers – 4700 in all. There were few delays. The worst occurred in Paris where a ground service vehicle hit the nose probe, bending it through 90 degrees. A new one, flown from Toulouse, was fitted in time to allow the aircraft to leave for Rio just seven hours late. About two-thirds of the way through this programme, on 7 July, our own flights started.

This route flying was to be done by airline methods, so it had been necessary to devise them. Our navigation and communications staff had produced documentation and had surveyed radio coverage. Trained flight planners, loading officers and maintenance engineers were waiting to try their newly acquired skills. Cabin crew were needed, too, but ours had been unable to agree their pay for the new type, so refused to take part. As a result, crews from Gulf Air, Singapore Airlines and Air India were invited to man the cabins. This they did with great enthusiasm, adding pleasantly exotic touches to the service, which was supervised by our own senior cabin staff.

G-BOAC, aircraft 204, was used for the route-proving. It was the first to be provided with a cabin fully equipped to British Airways' standards. Concorde's galleys are small, constrained by the narrow fuselage, so much thought had gone into their design, to allow the smooth service of up to a hundred meals. As is the case with all modern aircraft, food is pre-prepared in kitchens at the airport and put on board in special containers designed to fit stowage spaces in the galleys. Ovens heat up some of the dishes, and the meal service is done from wheeled trolleys, each of which hold a number of trays.

Entering the aircraft, through the front left-hand door, one can see the trolleys opposite, in their stowage spaces. They look a little odd for they appear to be tilted at an angle to the vertical. There is a good reason for what may seem to be bad joinery: the cabin, both on the ground and in the air, is at an angle of 3 to 5 degrees nose-up – the trays inside are level. Because of the angle, and also to counter the acceleration as the aeroplane climbs, the trolleys are equipped with a foot-operated brake, which prevents them from wandering off downhill while passengers are being served.

The interior appearance of Alpha Charlie was much more attractive than that of earlier models. The overhead luggage bins had been redesigned to provide better headroom, lighting had been improved and new seats installed. The whole cabin, although inevitably long and narrow, looked brighter, more roomy.

The design of aircraft interiors is taken very seriously by airlines – they almost invariably install their own seats and make their own choice of carpets, hangings and covering materials. The final selection from a number of competing designs is often made by the Board itself. The result is, after all, the most obvious projection of the airline's image to its customers. The decisions in Concorde's case show clearly that both Air France and British Airways were concerned chiefly to make the cabins undramatic – as much as possible like any other airliner's. Made, as they had to be, well before the start of scheduled services, the decisions were influenced by the concern that passengers might find the thought of supersonic travel alarming.

Warm, bright colours were chosen. Leather was rejected (although at the proving stage the front cabin of the Air France aircraft had club-style padded leather seats). The walls, ceilings and bulkheads were that bland, off-white-with-a-hint-of-texture so familiar to air travellers. The whole effect was one of reassurance. The Machmeter fitted to the front bulkhead of each cabin was the only indication that this was, in fact, an SST. Passengers have always enjoyed seeing the three digits change as we climb, and feel they're getting their money's worth when they see them reach 2·00.

Concorde's pleasant behaviour in service seems to provide all the reassurance needed. The interior of a second-generation SST might well look very different; the elegance of its shape, the exclusiveness of its speed might somehow be reflected in its cabin design. It's a pleasant idea to dream about, but in 1975 the mood was rather different. Supersonic flying was new to all but a very few people.

Our route-proving began, carrying invited passengers, with flights to Bahrain. The plan was to expand the area covered in two further phases, to include Singapore and Melbourne. Having flown my share of the first phase, under the supervision of the manufacturer's pilots, I moved to Kuala Lumpur, Malaysia, to await the extension of the route. A considerable team, led by John Cochrane, was already there.

The first of the new series of flights was to Bombay and Bahrain. The aircraft stood on the tarmac against a background of palm trees. With its outline slightly blurred by the early morning mist and its visor covered in condensation, it looked oddly vulnerable.

We burst out of cloud as we accelerated up past Sumatra, and flew briefly at Mach 2 between the Nicobar Islands and across the Bay of Bengal before decelerating to subsonic speed to cross India. Santa Cruz airport, Bombay, was as it always is just after dawn: fog lifting slowly, vultures wheeling above the *ghats* and a steep approach over the hills to the runway. Across India we had heard the morning shift of air traffic controllers calling on the VHF radio from tower to tower, as if to reassure themselves that no part of the continent had disappeared overnight.

Out of Bombay, for Bahrain, the aircraft was light – only about 140 tons for the flight of $1\frac{1}{4}$ hour's duration. We reached 60,000 feet in 18 minutes, still climbing rapidly before levelling out. It seemed that the wheels were hardly up before we saw the yellow coastline of Oman. Landing at Bahrain, in what was still the early morning, we were able to get away from the airport before the baking heat built up.

The flight pattern picked up speed, then, and Alpha Charlie shuttled rapidly between Bahrain, Kuala Lumpur and Singapore, keeping fairly close to schedule and shortening transit times as the ground crews became used to handling Concorde. On 4 August we made the first of a series of flights from Singapore to Melbourne. The route was almost a straight line from Singapore to the Great Australian Bight. Passing between Java and Bali, we could see the Indonesian islands stretched out for about 300 miles in each direction – mountains surrounded by building thunderclouds, purple and grey. After crossing the north-west coast of Australia between Broome and Port Hedland, we flew over the Great Sandy Desert, a brilliant pattern of russet waves looking unreal, like the contour shading of an atlas. The appearance of emptiness was accurate. The Australian authorities had calculated that less than a hundred people lived in the fifty-mile-wide swathe of country, a thousand miles long, centred on our track – and that most of those were transient, while the remainder lived in one homestead.

Out in the Bight, descent was begun as we turned around Kangaroo Island, off Adelaide. We passed subsonically over the Victorian farmlands and landed in a heavy shower at Melbourne. The flight was met by large crowds who had come to see the beautiful bird land, and by a wonderfully eccentric 'demo' – a youthful group of environmentalist opponents, in a novel form of protest, had occupied all the lavatories at the airport. The Australian press, which can be the most vindictive in the world when its hackles are up, reacted kindly. The *Australian* headlined its article, 'A Fair Go for the Concorde'. The *Melbourne Age* took a similar line: 'This is the time to give the 1300 mph snoop-nosed propelling pencil a fair go,' continuing, 'No amount of emotional flushing will wash away the fact that supersonic travel is just that – a fact.'

The rest of the programme went well. The aircraft performed

all that was asked of it, the aircrews gained experience, the ground crews refined their techniques. There was a final fortnight of trans-Atlantic crossings, to Gander, and the programme was complete: 130 flights, 380 hours and 6500 passengers – a formidable breaking-in. We had seen again the stratospheric temperature changes, which caused a problem with the cruise mode of the autopilot. In fact, it was now possible to pinpoint some of the places where they could be expected to be present – the northern Omani mountain area was one. Runway corrugations had not prevented any operations but we knew that that difficulty would have to be dealt with, too. However, in all temperatures, and on all routes, including the long one from Bahrain to Singapore, the aircraft performance came up to expectations. Fuel reserves appeared to be adequate, as predicted, and the crews got on well with the aircraft.

By mid-September we were thoroughly immersed in the enormously complicated task of getting the services started on the date which had now been agreed between the two governments: 21 January 1976. It had also been agreed, between the two airlines, that there would be no competition over who would be first into the air – instead, we would do it together. This could mean only one thing: a bravura performance on the inaugural day, something that had never been done before, simultaneous take-offs, from London and Paris. The challenge was accepted readily. A first study showed it should be quite possible, given detailed planning. We began to arrange it, cooperating with our colleagues in Air France.

There was also a great deal of work to do on preparing our procedures, documentation and training programme. All this had to lead, in good time, to the issue of an Air Operator's Certificate which would allow British Airways to fly Concorde commercially. There were a large number of threads to be pulled together, a large number of minor faults – revealed by the route-proving – to be put right, and an increasing need to become involved with the media. All members of the nucleus group set to work, each undertaking tasks somewhat outside the usual range of airline pilots' interests. Captain Tony Meadows did pioneer work on airport noise, out of which came the standard method used by both airlines ever since. Captain Chris Morley got to grips with the subtleties of the navigation system, and went to Syria with a government party to negotiate a suitable route. One pilot prepared the applications for low-visibility landings; others rewrote sections of the manuals.

The most important part of my job, apart from overseeing all this, was to make sure that the aircraft was fit for our crews to fly. I had learned early on in the development business that the fifteen years or so of an airliner's life reveal failings in design which tend not to show up on shorter assessments. In particular, any poor human engineering of instruments or systems which encouraged people to make mistakes would somehow seek the mistakes out. At the end of the route-proving Captain Norman Todd, the flight training manager, and I were asked to put together a report on the aircraft. It was made clear that the report should not be influenced by any considerations other than our own professional judgment. Among other things, we reported that the cruise autopilot was unsatisfactory for airline use.

Just why the manufacturers had refused to act on our earlier warnings on this subject is a mystery, but the fact is that they had. Their view seemed to be that the excursions caused by sudden temperature changes could be handled quite easily by well-trained pilots, and in a sense that was true. We were not sure, however, that this would *always* be the case, over many years, long after the glamour and excitement of the early flights had worn off. Just as importantly, we believed it wrong to distract the crew from their other tasks just to restore the aeroplane to its proper flight path.

It was a matter of judgment. Our Board let the government know they would not accept the aircraft in this condition, on the grounds that it did not meet the terms of its contract. There was a stormy meeting in Toulouse, and another before the Air Registration Board. In the end we agreed to start operations with a limited number of specially trained crews, over a restricted range of routes, on condition that an early solution was found. It was. In November I examined a first attempt, which was an improvement but still not good enough. Finally, in April 1976, I flew around the Bay of Bengal with Jean Franchi and Gilbert Defer of Aerospatiale looking for cumulo nimbus clouds in which we knew we would find large temperature shears. We saw then and proved an autopilot cruise mode which for ingenuity and elegance has no equal. It was quickly fitted.

9. First Services

Only two SSTs have ever flown: Concorde and the TU144. The Soviet aircraft made its first flight on 31 December 1968, a little more than two months before its rival's. The flight was also the first airborne test of its four Kusnetsov engines, in sharp contrast to the long period of flight testing of the Olympus, but it won for the Russians what they obviously wanted – the date in the history books. They secured another one when, on 26 December 1975, the TU144 entered what was described as scheduled commercial service, carrying freight and mail between Moscow and Alma Ata, in Kazakhstan – a distance of about 1860 miles.

The whole of the Soviet flight test programme had been carried out in great secrecy, but the aircraft made successive appearances at the Paris Air Show, in 1971, 1973, 1975 and again in 1977. By the second visit, the aircraft had been very largely redesigned. The wings had acquired more camber and twist, the engines had moved outboard, the fuselage had grown longer, and 'canards' or foreplanes had appeared behind the crew cabin. At the 1973 show the TU144, during a demonstration flight which followed a particularly impressive one by Concorde, went into a steep climb: too steep, it appeared. During the dive which followed, one of the wings broke away and the aircraft crashed, killing its five crew and eight people in a nearby village. Whatever caused the crash (the absence of a flight recorder made analysis impossible), it did not seem to be due to any fundamental fault since no major modifications were noticed on subsequent appearances.

In spite of the crash, development continued, and it was always assumed that the intention was to put the aircraft into service. The TU144 was, however, never seen as a serious competitor in the West. Soviet aircraft are built principally for the state airline, Aeroflot, and for client countries. This is in itself an enormous market, and there is no network of service to support sales outside their own area. Their engines, in particular, are not designed for the long periods between maintenance which make Western engines so productive. And one significant feature of the prototype remained on the developed aircraft – the turbofan engines. These might make the aircraft marginally more efficient than Concorde in the subsonic régime but would restrict its range over supersonic sectors such as the North Atlantic.

So the news that the TU144 was in service had a hollow ring to it. It did not seem to have any bearing on what we were doing. Whether it yet was, or ever would be, an airliner had yet to be demonstrated.

G-BOAC had gone back to the factory at Filton to be brought up to the latest modification standard after the route-proving. The next off the line, G-BOAA, was ready for acceptance at Fairford where all the flight testing had been done. The series of acceptance flights started in mid-December. The first was a four-hour flight out into the Atlantic to check that the aircraft met its performance guarantee – that it would deliver the goods in terms of range and payload. A team of our experts flew with us, taking measurements. Three more flights followed in early January 1976. During these we checked every system on the aircraft according to a carefully designed schedule, looking for flaws. We found some minor ones but they were all quickly put right. On 14 January, I was able to take delivery of our first Concorde.

Leaving Fairford, we made a circuit and flew fast above the runway as a salute to the people who had brought her to this point. Halfway across the airfield we lit the afterburners and pulled up into a steep climb, turning towards Heathrow. A short flight along the airways brought Alpha Alpha to her new home in British Airways' maintenance complex. White-overalled engineers came out to meet us as we taxied past our stately 747s. They would be fitting her out with special airline equipment over the next few days. In Air France's hangars at Charles de Gaulle there were already two aircraft being prepared – F-BVFA, which had arrived on 19 December, and F-BTSC which had followed on 6 January.

The strands of preparation had come together now, with just

a week to go, and we concentrated on planning the inaugural services. The two airlines agreed that, in case of any last-minute delay, each would wait for the other for twenty minutes after the scheduled departure time of 11.40 (12.40 Paris time). A link telephone line was to be opened between the two control towers at London and Paris. Precise timings were agreed so that both aircraft would be in position on their respective runways four minutes before the take-off time. A special frequency would be allocated for the tower controllers to broadcast a 30-second countdown, and the brakes of the two aircraft would be released at exactly the same time. Norman Todd and I had agreed that he would command the flight out, and I the one home. John Lidiard was to be the flight engineer. Captain Pierre Chanoine was to command the Air France flight, and he and Norman Todd would have a public conversation on the radio during the push-back after the engines had been started.

Inaugural day was a Wednesday. On the previous Sunday we returned from Toulouse where we had all been having some simulator practice. The plans hardly needed polishing any more – everybody knew precisely what he had to do during the hours leading up to the departure. The CAA had caused some last-minute revisions, insisting that their flight inspectors should fly with us on the flight deck. After a good deal of argument, they finally agreed to make Brian Trubshaw and John Cochrane temporary inspectors for the purpose. We were delighted to have them come along on the first services – they would be useful as well as good company.

There was one final note of suspense – it was not yet certain that the route over Lebanon and Syria would be open to us on the day. Alternative route plans were prepared, but if the fully supersonic route was closed an intermediate landing would be needed, and nobody wanted that. One could only, at this stage, hope for the best.

Leaving home, early in the morning of 21 January, I wondered how I felt. Oddly enough, I didn't seem to be excited. The time for that had passed. The weeks and months before this day had been so filled with planning and rehearsing that there was nothing left but to fly – to take an aeroplane from London to Bahrain. The excitement was now for other people: the passengers, the press, the public. I prayed for luck, though – however well-organized a flight may be, there is always the possibility of some idiotic fault which will upset everything. Just for a start, I hoped that my car wouldn't choose this day to break down.

At the airport, there were already signs of traffic building up. The weather was fine, with a westerly wind. In the office we gathered for a final discussion. The route appeared to be open but had not been confirmed officially, so we would have to decide in flight whether or not we could go straight on from the Mediterranean. A car took us over to the flight planning office in the central area of the airfield. Its driver, an old colleague who had been in the airline as long as any of us, was obviously pleased to be part of the occasion.

The passengers comprised a mixture of fare-payers and invited guests, and they were arriving at Terminal 3. British Airways had opened reservations for the flight in the previous October, but many requests for places had been received earlier than that. Lord and Lady Leathers headed the list, having booked twelve years before. The guests included the Duke of Kent, Peter Shore, Secretary of State for Trade, and Eric Varley, Secretary of State for Industry. Several distinguished figures from the aviation industry came, too. Among them were Sir Leonard Cheshire VC, Lord Boyd-Carpenter, Chairman of the CAA, and Sir George Edwards, former Chairman of BAC, who of all people had a right to be there – the aeroplane's very existence was in a large part due to him. There was also a substantial contingent from the press, who would write, film and broadcast during the flight.

In the operations room we examined the weather forecasts, the route briefing and the flight plan. In spite of the full load, with strong winds behind us, there was substantial excess fuel available, which Norman Todd gladly accepted to cover the possibility of the route closing in front of us. The weather *en route* and at Bahrain was good. When we were ready we went straight out to the aeroplane – a short walk away on stand Juliet 2 – to begin the pre-departure checks. It all seemed to us, insulated as we were from the popping flash-bulbs around the check-in desks, to be going very smoothly.

A reception was being held by the airline for guests, who would be able to watch the departure live and at the same time see the split-screen television presentation of the joint take-off.

A crowd which eventually numbered 3000 gathered on the roof of the Queen's Building. The airport perimeter roads were by now becoming jammed with parked cars.

At 10.50 the coats were loaded, and five minutes later the passengers began to board the aircraft. One of them, a Mr Bob Ingham, who had booked his ticket in 1969, appeared in a weird costume consisting of a white and purple cloak and head-dress, his face painted silver. To the appalled staff and delighted photographers he explained that it was 'a futuristic outfit for a futuristic aeroplane'. By 11.15 they were all on board. Soon after, two engines were started and we were pushed backwards out into the apron area. The second pair of engines started without a hitch. We were exactly on time. News came through that all was well at Charles de Gaulle.

The taxi out to runway 28 Left went a little too smoothly – we were in position a minute early at 11.35. When we arrived there were no other aircraft about, but a small queue built up while we waited for the countdown. It included Jumbos of Pan Am and TWA.

The countdown started. A final check around the instruments. It really was remarkable, but this aeroplane had not even one of the many small defects that can be carried. It was almost as if it were on its best behaviour. As if it knew . . .

'Three, two, one . . .'

Brakes released. Full power. Clock started. The engines all spooled up perfectly, the afterburners all lit up, all four green lights showed that everything was as it should be. It was a very normal take-off. We turned around to the south-east, towards the coast at Worthing, climbing up to 25,000 feet. As we reached our cruising altitude over the Channel, we heard that the Air France take-off had gone equally smoothly. It was estimated later that 250 million people watched the simultaneous take-off on television sets around the world. How anybody arrives at such a figure is beyond my understanding, but it certainly did not trouble us then – there was too much to do.

Flying across Europe, west of Paris, over Geneva towards Venice, we were subsonic. To the usual communications with air traffic control was added the broadcast interview with Norman Todd, which was relayed by the BBC. It took some time finding a radio frequency which would get us through to London. There was a continuous flow of people coming up to the flight deck to inspect the workers. Jimmy Andrew had come along to see this culmination of his efforts over many years and, as usual, he offered to help. He took up position at the rear of the cockpit and filtered the guests and cameramen through in as orderly a way as possible, answering many of their questions.

Approaching Venice, going through the transonic checklist, the flight deck emptied, and the atmosphere was a good deal easier. The passengers had started their lunch. We heard afterwards from the cabin crew that even the meal service had not quelled the excitement behind us. Everyone seemed to be taking pictures of everyone else. Microphones were out and tape-recorders buzzed. Aisles were blocked. People climbed over seats. Somehow the cabin crew, led by Jack Hawkins in the front cabin and John Hitchcock in the rear, managed to smile and serve their way through it all, and everybody who sat down for long enough got to eat and drink.

One hour and twenty minutes after take-off we were out over the sea and it was time to go supersonic. The throttles were opened to full power, the afterburners were re-lit. We climbed and accelerated rapidly. Half way down the Adriatic we reached Mach 2 at 50,000 feet. It had been clear across most of Europe, and here the view was splendid – the boot-shape of Italy stretching ahead on the right, with Brindisi on the heel and the Appenines ridging down the middle. Along the left side ranged the mountains of Yugoslavia, Albania and then Greece, all in view at the same time; ahead was our exit through the Strait of Otranto.

We shot out into the Mediterranean, watched Mounts Olympus and Parnassus slide by, and entered a left turn around the south of Crete. Here, from 56,000 feet up, the clear horizon showed the earth's curvature as we moved towards the darkening eastern sky. Now we found the workload was building up. Because the various air traffic control systems along the route were unaccustomed to handling supersonic aircraft, we had arranged for them all to be properly briefed by our own specialists beforehand. In theory, all the controllers would know exactly what to expect and how to deal with Concorde. In fact their supervisors seemed to have kept the subject a close secret. Reporting-points – the position at which an aircraft must tell air traffic control where it is – came thicker and faster. At each change to a new control authority our reported altitude caused disbelief; our time to the next checkpoint was assumed to be an error. Patiently and, I hope, politely, we explained the situation to each controller – after all, it was hardly his fault that no one had told him about this odd vehicle. It all took up much too much air-time but it paid dividends later. Each successive flight became easier as the controllers got to know us.

Our worries about the Syrian airspace evaporated – we were accepted without question. We had passed around the south of Cyprus and were in a long, wide arc over Syria when the sun set abruptly behind us. The aeroplane was now at 60,000 feet in cold air – about $-70°C$. Following a track some twenty-five miles south of the main oil pipeline from the Arabian Gulf to the Mediterranean, we raced down the home stretch. The gas-flares of the Saudi Arabian oil wells began to fill the space below – each one appearing, even from this height, to light up a halo of dust. Calculating on a slight tailwind, we started the descent 280 miles from Bahrain.

As we descended, it became increasingly clear that the tail-wind was stronger than expected, and that the cold air was producing more thrust from the idling engines than would let us down in time to make a straight-in approach to runway 12, the one in use. So reverse thrust was selected, increasing the rate of descent. It soon got us back on to the right flight path. The island of Muharraq was visible through the visor. Twenty-five miles out, the nose was lowered to 5 degrees, and the runway came into view in the now-unobstructed windscreen. So did the Visual Approach Slope Indicators (VASIs) – angled red and white lights on each side of the touchdown point which confirmed we were on the glideslope. The wheels were lowered and the landing check completed. All that was needed now was for Norman to drive the aeroplane down the approach and land it – something he had done often enough before, and no doubt rehearsed in his mind a few times in the last few days.

We touched down at 15.17 GMT – three hours and thirty-seven minutes from brake-release at London. A few minutes later we were at the terminal building and the passengers were leaving. Some shouted congratulations from the other end of the narrow passage which leads to the flight deck. To us, unbuckling our straps, unlatching our minds from the concentration of the last hours, congratulations seemed at first a little incongruous. We had done nothing extraordinary – had simply flown the aircraft from London to Bahrain. This flight had been the end product of years of preparation. It had been hard work, and there had been tension – we were feeling it drain away now. But the tension was purely extraneous, caused by the enormous expectations which centred on a single flight. Now it was over,

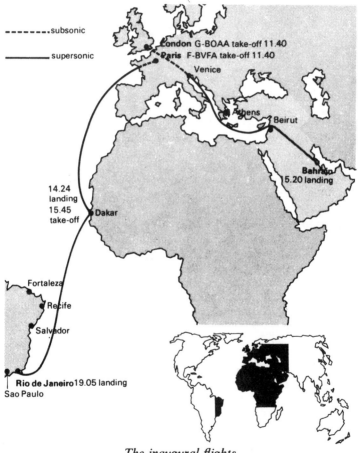

- - - - - - -. subsonic

――――――― supersonic

London G-BOAA take-off 11.40
Paris F-BVFA take-off 11.40
Venice
Athens
Beirut
Bahrain
15.20 landing
14.24 landing
15.45 take-off
Dakar
Fortaleza
Recife
Salvador
Rio de Janeiro 19.05 landing
Sao Paulo

The inaugural flights

successfully, we imagined that our flights would settle down to a more normal pattern. We shut down the systems, one by one, tidied up the paperwork and handed the aeroplane over for the night.

The whole crew, along with all the passengers, had been invited by the Ruler to a celebratory banquet. We assembled in a vast anteroom where formal introductions were made and spiced Arabian coffee was served. Here we met many of the passengers for the first time and had a chance to share in their excitement. After a while we moved to the dining room where numerous robed servants stood behind tables covered with dishes. Kebabs sat on beds of rice, vegetables were laid out in patterns, fruits were piled high. In front of my place lay most of a lamb, barbecued. I could hardly wait to set upon it – we had not had time to eat during the flight and were beginning to notice our hunger. Later, grateful to the Ruler for his welcome and for our first square meal of the day, we moved on to a second reception at the Gulf Hotel, and finally, with relief, to our beds.

In the meantime, Concorde F-BVFA, operating as Flight AF085, had reached Rio de Janeiro via Dakar. There had been emotional scenes at the send-off party at Charles de Gaulle Airport. The flight's guest-list included Marcel Cavaillé, the Transport Minister, and passengers joined the aircraft from the USA, Germany, Italy, Sweden, Spain, Switzerland and Brazil. The crew had encountered just one technical problem: out of Dakar, a secondary air door – which opens to allow cooling air to flow around the engines in supersonic flight – had failed to open, delaying the acceleration through Mach 1.

The two flights had been successes – no one could deny that. Concorde was in service.

The return flight, the next morning, was much less public, but in technical terms it was a good deal more interesting. The same strong westerly winds over Europe which had given us such a fast flight time on the way to Bahrain were still present – as headwinds of up to 150 miles per hour. The flight plan showed we would need all the fuel we could get on board to give us adequate reserves on arrival at London. As much fuel as possible would have to be carried in the rear trim tank. Although some of it would be used during the taxi, so as to get the centre of gravity properly placed, it would still be nearly full on take-off.

Getting airborne from Bahrain, we were able to pick up speed quickly, as the take-off path is directly over the sea and therefore no noise-abatement technique is required. By the time we had reached 5000 feet altitude we were climbing at an indicated speed of 400 knots, the nose and visor up. We reached 25,000 feet and Mach 0·93 nine minutes after take-off. At this point, the main centre of gravity transfer has to start, shifting fuel back into the rear trim tank. We soon discovered that there was not enough room in the trim tank to receive it, and the much slower process of reducing the fuel in the forward trim tanks, by burning it in the engines, could not cope with our rate of acceleration.

Anticipating what later became a formal technique, we levelled out for a while, until enough fuel had been burned off to permit the rest of the transfer to take place. About ten minutes of subsonic flight dealt with the problem. We wondered, briefly, if we had miscalculated in some way, but we hadn't – it was just that, amazingly enough, the particular combination of circumstances which applied to this flight had never occurred before, even on proving flights.

Returning by day over the route we had covered the previous night, we soon established Mach 2. Norman Todd, who had changed places with me, was doing the explaining on the radio. It was all a little easier, and we managed to have a brief lunch. Almost too soon, it was time to descend along the Adriatic, slowing to subsonic speed before reaching Venice. As we crossed Austria and Switzerland, it became clear that the winds were not as unfavourable as had been forecast – there would be plenty of fuel left at London. French, then British air traffic control took over, and we landed at Heathrow six minutes late – not bad considering the headwinds. The passengers clapped.

There was the inevitable press conference afterwards, from which we slipped away for a debriefing with our colleagues who had helped to prepare the flight. And then home, tired, but filled with a sense of satisfaction that we had brought off this spectacular double inaugural. There was regular flying to look forward to, now – that was a happy thought.

10. The Battle for the USA

Twelve days after the two aircraft returned home to London and Paris, William T. Coleman Jr, the Secretary of Transportation, published his decision on Concorde's entry into the United States. It was the beginning of the final phase of a struggle which was to continue, in a series of set-pieces and skirmishes, for another twenty months.

The campaign against Concorde in the USA was powerful and unremitting, for its origins lay in the extraordinary history – tragic or triumphant according to viewpoint, but traumatic in any case – of the country's own SST programme. Launched in 1963 by President Kennedy, at a time when American endeavours in space were at last beginning to show signs of catching up with the Soviet Union's, the competition to produce a supersonic airliner led to intense work by Boeing, Lockheed and North American. Prospects were encouraging. In order to reserve their places on whichever production line would finally build it, many airlines (including TWA, Pan American and, later, BOAC) took out options – a revealing expression of confidence in the US aircraft industry.

North American dropped out of the race but the two remaining designs emerged in 1966. Boeing's, the 2707-100, was the most advanced, even revolutionary. It employed swing-wings which, when they were moved backwards, formed an extended delta shape for high-speed flight. When swung forward, they became conventional, mildly swept wings which would improve take-off and landing performance. Two other features made this an astonishingly bold design: the aircraft was designed to fly at Mach 3, and to carry approximately 300 passengers. The passenger capacity would make it more than twice Concorde's size, and the speed would mean that conventional aircraft alloys could not be used for the major part of the structure, so titanium, much more difficult to work, would predominate.

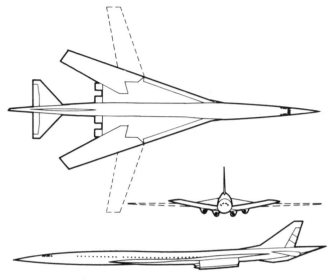

Boeing 2707-100

Lockheed's design was much less radical – a double-angled slender delta wing and narrow fuselage were intended to carry around 200 passengers. It looked very like a larger version of Concorde but, like the 2707, it promised higher speeds and greater range.

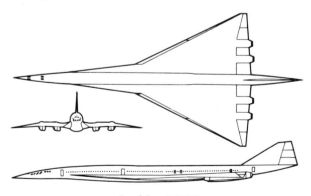

Lockheed SST

The Boeing design caught the imagination of the judges, and in December 1966 it was selected. The airlines, too, liked the look of the 2707. The list of option-holders grew, continuing to exceed Concorde's. But the design kept running into problems, mainly to do with weight. The swing-wings moved on two enormous hinges, whose weight was supposed to be more than cancelled out by the increases in lift. Because flaps were necessary on the extended wings, the engineering complexity grew. Canards were added on a new version, designated the 2707-200, but in the end it had to be admitted that there was no solution – that even the most successful aircraft company in the world could not make the swing-wing work at this size and speed. All this took two years and a great deal of money.

In January 1969 (just after the TU144's first flight – just before 001's), the final version was announced – the 2707-300. The aircraft now looked more like all the other competitors, except that the wing was of a higher aspect ratio, and there was a tail-plane, or horizontal stabilizer. This looked an extremely promising design. Its engineering was comparatively simple. In theory, the wing would give it better performance than Concorde's in subsonic cruise, and the combination of wing and

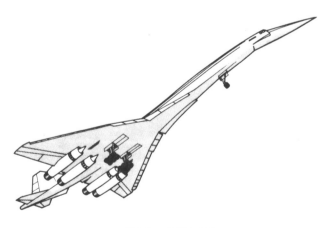

Boeing 2707-300

engine would produce lower noise on take-off. On the other hand, the cruising speed was now down to Mach 2·7, and the passenger load had reduced to 230 or so.

While the project was taking up thousands of man- and computer-hours, the forces of opposition had been growing around two separate groups: those who disapproved of government funding of the project, and those who feared that SSTs were an environmental disaster. The first group, whose principal activist was Senator Proxmire, was determined that if the project was worth pursuing at all then it should be supported by private capital. As it clearly couldn't be, then it should be stopped. The environmentalists represented in many ways some of the fundamental aspirations of the 1960s. Composed very largely of fairly affluent, middle-class people – often academics – they sought a cleaner, kinder world in which industrial growth would no longer be an end in itself. Improving the quality of life – including that of other people's lives, for 'concern' was very much part of the new ethic – would replace more worldly ambitions.

The two groups were agreed in their opposition to the SST, in spite of the fact that they were rather odd allies. The defenders of the nation's taxpayers, who worked so effectively in Congress, were not necessarily the sort of people who would spend much time protecting the habitat of a rare and threatened species of bird, whereas the environmentalists would actively encourage government spending on projects of which they approved. But on this subject they were united. The SST must be killed.

Formidable ammunition was provided for this powerful combination of interests when the report of a commission set up by President Nixon was published in October 1970. Its findings were extremely unfavourable, principally on financial grounds, but it also included a frightening list of possible environmental hazards. Interestingly, in the light of subsequent events, the report, as well as dealing with the US SST, included suggestions for bringing the Concorde project to an end by noise regulation.

Environmentalist groups formed in profusion. The most vociferous, the Citizens League Against the Sonic Boom, had been formed in 1967 by Dr William Shurcliff, a Harvard scientist. His and other groups now combined to form the Coalition Against the SST which, on 5 March 1970, placed a full-page advertisement in the *New York Times*, headlined in bold lettering:

SST AIRPLANE OF TOMORROW
BREAKS WINDOWS, CRACKS WALLS, STAMPEDES CATTLE
AND WILL HASTEN THE END OF THE
AMERICAN WILDERNESS

The rest of the advertisement, in closely printed paragraphs, set out a wonderfully imaginative list of disasters that would, or might, happen if any SST were ever allowed to fly.

Support came from Europe, too. In Britain, sections of the press saw the Concorde programme as a public scandal. Estimates of the programme's cost had grown so frighteningly that either the various governments must have been incompetent – which was bad enough – or they must have deliberately misled Parliament and the public – which was worse. Mary Goldring of the *Economist* concentrated on the financial aspects, while Andrew Wilson produced a series of articles in the *Observer* exploring the environmental issues as well. A retired schoolteacher named Richard Wiggs formed the Anti-Concorde Project to publicize the views of all who felt threatened by what seemed to them a sinister plot to pursue a grandiose scheme at their expense.

Many British Concorde opponents were invited to give evidence bearing on the US SST programme, at hearings of a Senate sub-committee chaired by Senator Proxmire. They managed, between them, to give the impression that Concorde had little chance of surviving the British public's hostility – news which was important to Congressmen whose minds were not yet made up. Many liberal Democrats held the view that spending on the SST would deprive other, more socially important programmes, and some Republicans believed, like Proxmire, that if the SST was worth building, Wall Street would fund it. But a majority of both parties felt that since the British and French governments were helping Concorde's manufacturers then they should help Boeing. If, however, it could be shown that Concorde was going to die, then the SST's life-support system of government funds could be switched off.

Not only did British appearances before the Proxmire committee have some influence there but they also had a reciprocal effect at home. The committee's proceedings were widely reported in Britain as if they were part of an impartial inquiry – such as is expected from a Royal Commission. They most certainly were not. Nor, in the United States, are the activities of such committees expected to be impartial: they are often a means for their members, and in particular their chairmen, to influence the policies of the Executive.

The battle for the US SST was finally fought out in Congress, over the appropriation of funds for continuing the programme. There was lobbying by one side, filibustering by the other. The press were firmly on the side of cancellation, and Congressmen were receiving significant numbers of letters from their electors. In the end, on the night of 19 May 1971, by a majority of 49 votes to 47, the American SST died.

It seems clear, with hindsight, that the issue of government funding was the most respectable of those that tipped the balance. Projects which rely heavily on new technology have a way of escalating in cost – a tendency which should be predictable by those who start them. The environmental issue seemed powerful at the time, and surely had some influence on the decision, but it has since been shown to have been largely based on misapprehension. The Climatic Impact Assessment Program, which employed over a thousand scientists worldwide, reported favourably in 1975 on the effect of a much larger fleet of SSTs than, by then, was ever likely to fly. Much of the 'evidence' of environmental damage used in the campaign to kill the SST was hypothetical. The fact that the hypotheses often came from scientists of distinguished reputation lent them credence they did not deserve.

The assumption that the Concorde project would fail continued – for the next two years there was little discussion of the subject in the American press. In January 1973 Pan American and TWA cancelled their Concorde options. Neither airline was in good shape financially – they had made heavy investments in their new 747 fleets and the market had not yet caught up. The chances of a return on Concorde's price seemed to them too slim, despite the fact that the aircraft was technically successful and was meeting its standards of performance. The action of these two major airlines (and a number of others followed in cancelling their options) seemed to be the final blow for the Anglo-French SST, but it stubbornly refused to go away.

Worse than that, it actually dared to come to the USA – to the opening ceremonies at the new Dallas–Fort Worth Airport, Texas, in 1973. BAC and Aerospatiale had adopted a low profile in the United States after the dramas of 1971, but now they decided to assert Concorde's existence and viability. Now, also, they had an aeroplane they could show off. Aircraft 02, the second pre-production model, was fitted with the new, 'clean' version of the Olympus engine. The prototypes had done little for their image, in the face of all the environmental fears, by trailing clouds of smoke behind them. The virtually smokeless 02 was greeted rapturously at Dallas. On the return journey it carried a full load, equivalent to 100 passengers and their baggage, from Washington to Paris – an impressive demonstration of its capabilities.

From this time until the end of 1974, successive visits to Boston, Miami, Los Angeles, San Francisco and Anchorage showed the aircraft to the American public and won far more approval than rejection. Huge crowds – in Los Angeles an estimated 250,000 – turned out to see it. Reports in the press, with the notable exceptions of some of the traditionally liberal east coast papers, were generally balanced and fair.

Concorde was due to start operations towards the end of 1975, and it was vital that it should be able to fly the routes between the European capitals and New York – the centre of American trade and an historic gateway to the whole country. Between 60 and 70 per cent of the passengers originating in Europe still used New York as their first point of entry, although the percentage had declined since the end of the Second World War. The routes also carried something like 40 per cent of all international travellers. Concorde was important to New York, as well, for in a period of economic decline it could ill afford to lose a further proportion of the business which flowed through its airports.

But New York suffered from aircraft. John F. Kennedy Airport, which, when it was known as Idlewild, existed peacefully in marshland, was now surrounded on most sides by growing suburbs. The residents complained as only New Yorkers know how. Local associations fought to curtail operations, to ban noisy aircraft, even to move the airport. The growing influence of special interest groups gave them instant access to the media, and politicians, actual or aspiring, raced to take advantage of this new source of power. Then it began to dawn on them that Concorde was coming.

To bring matters to a head, British Airways and Air France, in February 1975, filed with the FAA an amendment to their operating specifications, announcing formally their intentions to operate Concorde to Washington and New York. This procedure, normally a technical matter, is required of any foreign airline intending to change the type of aircraft it is is using into any US airport. It allows the FAA to inspect the airline's procedures and to be sure they are in compliance with US domestic laws. On this occasion, the amendment was intended to remove any lingering doubts about the determination of the airlines to operate Concorde to New York, and to trigger a response from the US authorities.

By law, any agency of the US government must file an Environmental Impact Statement (EIS) with the White House's Council of Environmental Quality before committing what is termed 'a significant Federal act'. Allowing Concorde to land in America, after the debate over the US SST, was seen as such an act, and so, in March, the Department of Transportation published a draft EIS for Concorde. Over the next month, hearings on it were held by the FAA.

By now, the vast majority of Congressmen were aware that the number of Concordes likely to be built could hardly pose, even on the worst assumptions, any real threat to the atmosphere. They could also see that banning the aircraft would be harmful to international relations. Conversely, supporting the entry of a foreign SST when they had helped to cancel their own could make them unpopular with some of their voters. So Congress, almost to a man, adopted a hands-off attitude.

This vacuum of opinion in Congress caused the battle to shift to the EIS hearings. The draft statement, with the benefit of the mass of research work carried out since the 1971 decision, concluded that there was insufficient evidence of environmental impact to deny the airlines their Concorde services. At the hearings the opponents again made their contributions which, by now, included some undisguised examples of xenophobia among the more familiar economic and environmental arguments. One polite, but misinformed, old lady provided her own highly individual comment. She explained at length that what really worried her was the sonic boom. When, eventually, the chairman dared to point out that sonic booms over land were illegal, she replied, 'It's illegal to fly into mountains, but they do.' There was no answer to that, so, in due course, the Department of Transportation retired to produce the final EIS, and to make a decison, based on its contents, on whether Concorde should be allowed into the United States. It seemed likely that the decision would be favourable.

It would still be a difficult political action. Washington's Dulles Airport was Federally owned, and therefore under the jurisdiction of the Department, but JFK was not – and the opposition there, to all forms of aircraft noise and pollution, was intense. New York State's Governor Carey asked the Port of New York and New Jersey Authority, which operated JFK, to ban Concorde until what he described as 'environmental concerns' were satisfactorily settled. The administration of President Ford tried hard to persuade the British and French to be content with permission only for Dulles. They suggested that, as this would clearly cause a diversion of traffic from New York, the city would in due course come round. The airlines were unimpressed.

Under the terms of the Chicago Convention of 1946, which governs all international air transport, all 133 signatories have the right to operate their aircraft into each other's countries. Concern about engine noise from the early American subsonic jets had not prevented Britain and France from allowing them into their airports. Concorde was in the process of being cleared, by an elaborate and thoroughly democratic process, from the accusations made against it. There seemed no reason, in equity or common sense, why it should be held up any longer. But the whole process dragged out into the fall of the year. Discussions between the airlines and the Port Authority were wholly unproductive, and the Department of Transportation seemed unwilling to provoke a crisis between the Federal government and the State of New York by publishing the final EIS.

At this stage, in a manner typical of Concorde's turbulent

history, the whole structure of patient negotiation was exploded by an intervention from outside. The Greater London Council, perhaps infected by the classic Federal-State battle developing in the United States, chose to play politics with Concorde's noise.

During the route-proving, which ended in September 1975 extensive noise monitoring had been carried out at Heathrow Airport by the CAA and the Department of Trade. Our procedures were by no means fully developed by that time, and some of the flights were used to demonstrate specific performance features, producing considerably more noise than they normally would. In spite of these factors, the figures looked quite promising to us, showing a marked improvement towards the end of the series.

But some members of the GLC were pressing the government to pay for double-glazing on the windows of recently built houses near Heathrow ...

The GLC commissioned its own Environmental Sciences Group to carry out their own study of Concorde's effect on London. The group set up 46 monitoring stations around Heathrow and set to work. Their thoroughly researched report produced conclusions which were, in general, unfavourable. However, within their terms of reference, it was fair. Unfortunately, it needed expert interpretation to show that in practice the effects on Heathrow's neighbours would not be as bad as it indicated, and that its conclusions were not directly applicable to American airfields and, in particular, to New York.

The council did not immediately publish the report. Instead it prepared a press release which ignored the report's carefully worded conclusions, and selected those pieces of explanatory data which would have the greatest impact. One member of the study group was so alarmed by what he saw happening to his scientifically prepared information that he telephoned BAC to warn them. They didn't believe him.

The news, when it finally came out, was that Concorde was three times louder than the 707, six times louder than the L-1011 ... This came as something of a surprise to most of the public living around Heathrow, but it was, understandably, reported with glee across the Atlantic. The *Washington Post* saw it as dooming any prospects of Concorde being allowed into JFK.

The credibility of all previous statements by the manufacturers and airlines — even of the draft EIS — was destroyed overnight. After all, would the Greater London Council so violently attack the home product unless it was truly awful?

Naturally enough, Secretary Coleman's decision was delayed. In November the EIS was finally published, and he announced at a press conference that he would hold a further public hearing on 5 January 1976. In his statement he set out concisely all the issues which would affect his decision, and invited discussion on them.

December produced some more surprises. The least pleasant of them was the publication of a study by the Environmental Protection Agency of the noise effect of the proposed Concorde operations at Dulles. Like the GLC's report, this one demonstrated an odd lack of understanding of noise data. It was so damaging that the British Embassy took the unusual step of holding a press conference to refute the claims of an agency of the US government. Sandy Gordon-Cumming, the Embassy's civil aviation counsellor, made a powerful opening speech which listed four specific criticisms:

> First, the contours which purport to show the noise effect of Concorde do not in fact show the effect of a single Concorde take-off or landing at Dulles but the effect that would be produced by all seven likely take-off and landing patterns. This is about as meaningful as drawing a contour for a single heavy truck covering the whole of the United States because it could in theory drive on any road in the United States.
>
> Second, the effect of Concorde has been compared by the EPA with the noise of heavy down-town traffic (an inaccurate noise comparison anyway, as I shall explain later). This kind of noise is, of course, by definition a continuous noise. In fact Concorde will only fly to Dulles twice and day and, unlike other aircraft, not in the night hours, and people will only be exposed to its noise for a period of less than two minutes during the day.
>
> Third, the contours extending all the way to Baltimore rest on the assumption that Concorde will invariably be held down for air traffic reasons to a maximum height of 7000

feet. This assumption is quite unwarranted; air traffic controllers will, as with other aircraft, permit Concorde to climb to operating height as soon as possible.

Lastly, it is very evident that the EPA have confused two kinds of noise measurements commonly used for different purposes. In trying to describe the effect of the noise level in their contours they have therefore been grossly inaccurate. 90 EPNdB is approximately equivalent to 77dBA. This is not the noise level of a heavy truck or heavy street traffic; it is the noise level produced by a range of ordinary household appliances.

There, again, was the now-traditional confusion – this time between dBA and EPNdB. The assumption that the aircraft would fly at 7000 feet all the way to Baltimore was particularly amateurish. All published departure clearances end at a given altitude at which the pilot levels out if further instructions have not been received, in case of radio failure or temporary overloading of the system. Five minutes' conversation with any airline pilot would have clarified the author's mind. Everyone associated with the Concorde project was by now used to this sort of thing from propagandists, but we all found it strange coming from professionals.

Damage of this sort, even if well-countered, sticks. In the same month the House of Representatives voted for a six-month ban on Concorde flights to all US airports except Dulles. Not in itself effective, until ratified by the Senate, and in any case constitutionally doubtful, this vote indicated that the debate had reached the political level again. In fact it had, by now, the makings of an international incident.

Perhaps for this reason, the Concorde witnesses at the Coleman hearings were led by junior ministers of the British and French governments – possibly the first time that ministers had given evidence at a domestic public hearing held by another government. The hearing was notable, to me at any rate, because of the intervention of PATCO, the Professional Air Traffic Controllers' Organization, which raised doubts about Concorde's fuel reserves – an old question – and the ability of the US air traffic control system to handle Concorde – an entirely new one. This particular body was trying at the time to improve the pay and conditions of its members. To do so it claimed, quite correctly, that controllers'- responsibilities had grown and were continuing to do so. Unfortunately, they could not resist the temptation to include Concorde in the argument, and to claim, quite incorrectly, that it would require all sorts of extra efforts by controllers. This blow seemed particularly below the belt, coming, as it did, from an organization which included many old friends who understood aircraft.

On 4 February, Secretary Coleman delivered his decision. In a carefully worded, sometimes sonorous, always authoritative judgment, he covered all the arguments. He found many of the claims against Concorde either untrue or unproven and granted a sixteen-month trial period of operations to Dulles and JFK – one a day to Washington and two a day to New York for each airline. The trial would be monitored, and the results of the first twelve months' data collection would be used to determine whether the flights could continue or not.

The compromise of a trial period was perfectly. acceptable to the airlines – they were sure the aircraft would pass the test. The leader of the Environmental Defense Fund, John Hellegers, was at the press conference at which the announcement was made. Before even reading the 54-page section on the reasons for the decision – or the 37 pages of appendices – he telephoned a colleague, instructing him to file papers in court to overturn the decision.

The decision was powerful enough to withstand such attempts, but it contained one significant qualification, which appeared in a footnote. Referring to JFK, whose operators are the Port of New York and New Jersey Authority, Coleman pointed out 'that under federal policy that has hitherto prevailed, a local airport proprietor has had authority under certain circumstances to refuse landing rights'. He went on to imply that if the Port Authority refused the trials at JFK, and those at Dulles were successful, then Federal authority might finally be brought to bear on the Port. But it was only an implication.

What the Port feared most about Concorde was its noise. Airports all around the nation were being saddled with huge damage claims over their existing noise. If Concorde was really worse than the other aeroplanes the situation could become disastrous. Noise rules emanated from Washington, but the airport operators got all the flak. The Port was determined to try to shift the responsibility back to the Federal government – if they ordered the Port Authority to accept Concorde, they would have to accept the lawsuits, too.

The way was now open, however, for flights to Washington. Planning started for what, it was decided, would be another spectacular – this time a joint arrival. We agreed that on this occasion the British Airways flight would land first – simultaneous landings were a little too much to expect. The task, then, was to arrange for the two aircraft to cross the Atlantic in trail. To do this, it was necessary to work back from the point at which the two routes, from Paris and London, joined at 12 degrees west longitude. At this point there would have to be a gap of twelve minutes – about 300 miles – between the two aircraft: the minimum allowable separation on our track. This could be reduced when, on the other side, we started to descend. By varying the techniques we could close the gap to eight minutes or so. During the run past Philadelphia and Baltimore we could close it further, so that by the time we reached the final approach there would only be a few miles between us.

We discovered that because of the rather longer subsonic segment on the early part of the route from London a gap of seven minutes between the two take-offs would produce the required result at 12 degrees west, provided we both took off in the same direction. If the runway directions at the two airports were opposite (and this sometimes happens) a further five minutes would need to be added or subtracted. So, according to the situation on the day, the interval between the take-offs would need to be two, seven or twelve minutes. It needed a little coordinating, but it was quite possible.

Preparation for the show-business side of the operation included filming, and interviews with the press and televison. We had all become quite used to this by now, and it had contained some entertaining moments for me, such as appearing on the Shirley Bassey show, but this was serious stuff, with American television crews coming over to collect the sights and sounds of the real thing. I began to understand, from their questions, the total misapprehension of even such simple things as the aircraft's size which existed across the ocean. Safety kept cropping up, and the pilots were the best people to answer such questions

– after all, neither Norman Todd nor I looked much like people who would fly dangerous aeroplanes. It all took up a good deal of time, but we felt it was worth it if it helped to dispel some of the illusions.

There was much real operational work to be done, too – in among acceptance flights, autopilot tests (in Kuala Lumpur) and trips to Bahrain. A series of meetings was held with the FAA on the routes we would fly in the US airspace, and on the procedures the controllers would use for handling us. The people we dealt with were all old hands in the aviation business, and, under other circumstances, the meetings would have been pleasant, practical affairs. But political pressures were putting them in a difficult position. The final attacks on Concorde, at the February hearings, had raised the issue of special handling for Concorde. It was claimed that this grossly inflexible machine would, in effect, need all other aircraft cleared from its path, so that it could be brought straight in to its destination. Our answer, which was quite correct, was that Concorde could behave exactly like subsonic jets, except that its speed on final approach was a little higher. Therefore no special procedures would be needed. This was interpreted literally.

But, in fact, all aircraft have special needs. No one expected the jets, when they first arrived, to fly in holding patterns at the same speed as piston-engined aircraft. They simply couldn't. But Concorde could fly at the same speed as the subsonics, and so it had to. At least it had to until we demonstrated in the simulator, and even on the aircraft – circling over Land's End – that we could fly at our preferred speeds and still remain within the airspace protected for the patterns. We did it, incidentally, with the aid of a small circular slide-rule which was very quickly produced for us by Robert Pooley of Airtour International whose business is normally concerned with light aircraft. With it, we are able to steer and time the patterns precisely enough to stay within the reserved areas.

Concorde did not demand any more spacing behind it than the Jumbos (when they went into service the whole system of sequencing aircraft for approach was changed). Nor did Concorde need runway extensions, reinforcement of taxiways or new equipment for the terminals. But it was a fast machine, and flying it slowly cost fuel. Anything that could be done to straighten out routes and keep it flying fast for as long as possible, would be welcome. The FAA officials were as fair as they could be, but the distinction between 'special procedures' and a reasonable accommodation of a new aircraft was too fine to be understood in the *furore* surrounding the coming operation.

A good example of the result was the route into and out of Washington. The problem was caused by a reservation of airspace for testing military aircraft. These areas were designed

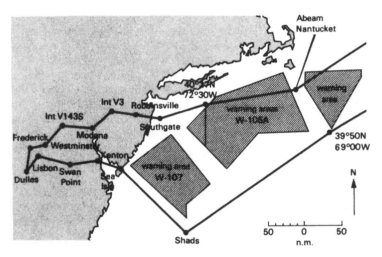

Routes in and out of Washington

around the subsonic routes, along the US coast and out towards Bermuda and the Caribbean. A supersonic aircraft needs to fly off the coast as long as possible, so our route, inbound, would have to be over W-105A, whose top was at 50,000 feet. On the way back to Europe we would have to skirt W-107, which extended to unlimited heights. The outbound route was simply an expensive bore – it involved flying 180 miles at right angles to our intended route before we could join it. The route in, however, presented something of a challenge, for it meant that we would have to cross 72°30′ west at 52,000 feet to produce the required separation from the zone, and then descend to become subsonic at 39,000 feet some 40 miles before the coast. Quite a small shift of the area's north-western boundary would accommodate our normal descent path, but it was not available – it would be a special procedure.

So, once more, we found a way round, or rather over.

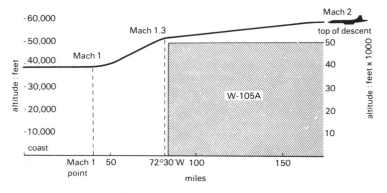

The descent into Washington

The pilots themselves designed, with, again, the help of the simulator, a technique which would cope with the squeeze between the position at which we were clear of the warning area and the Mach 1 point. The actual technique wasn't very difficult – from 52,000 feet down to about 43,000 feet a constant Mach number – 1·3 – was flown. At this point the autopilot began to capture the preset altitude of 39,000 feet, and the Mach number fell off to ·95, the subsonic cruising speed. The difficult part was to get to 52,000 feet, exactly, at 72°30′ west. The end-of-cruise altitude might be anything between 56,000 and 59,000 feet, and the wind component and air temperature (particularly the latter) affected the distance required. A simple series of graphs did the trick.

The procedure was aptly called the 'fall off the wall'. It worked beautifully. It is hard to describe the pleasure it gives a pilot to be able to throttle back, at a precise moment, the engines which are propelling over 100 tons of aircraft at 22 miles a minute, and then watch, checking progress on the graph, as it proceeds to slow down and descend to exactly the right height at exactly the right place. Air traffic controllers told me afterwards that they used to watch fascinated as the altitudes (which are transmitted from the aircraft and displayed on their screens) rolled off.

There were other subjects discussed with the FAA, other areas in which it became clear we would have to comply with every regulation for subsonic aircraft. They did offer to help when they could. Controllers would give us direct routeings, as they do to other aircraft, cutting off the corners of the airways when traffic permitted. They would even clear us through the reserved airspace, if it was known to be empty, but not on any planned basis, so that we could take advantage of it in fuel and payload calculations. In due course, it all came together, and the operation appeared to be quite satisfactory. In British Airways we decided that, at least until we had more knowledge of how the route worked in practice, we would limit the payload on westbound flights to about 80 passengers.

A few days before the inaugural flight, I went to Washington for the last of these meetings and found myself with a programme of interviews as well. Some were quite grand (nationwide networked TV programmes), but my favourite, and the most revealing, was a session on Fred Fiske's Empathy Show – a late-night talk-in broadcast from WWDC radio station. A tall antenna identified the modest buildings which housed the offices and studios. Tom Craft, our public relations manager, and I had a hamburger in a nearby diner as we waited for my scheduled 45-minute appearance to start at 10 pm.

It went on until one o'clock in the morning. Calls came in over the telephone, at first asking all the old questions, expressing all the old fears. A few of the callers were obviously members of one or other anti-SST group – their questions tended to be preceded by speeches I had heard before. Gradually, real questions began to appear from people who believed what they read in the papers and were worried. They listened to the answers.

About halfway through, an old lady rang in to declare her certainty that what the British were really up to was no less than the re-taking of Virginia and Maryland. Fiske managed to get rid of her rather too quickly for my liking – I was enjoying the idea. After that, there was a short pause. Perhaps listeners all over the District of Columbia were pondering this dramatic picture. Then the questions took a new turn. Why shouldn't it be given a chance? How can we tell what it's like if we don't see and hear it for ourselves? I could only agree.

Finally, at around midnight, I began to hear from supporters – people who were fairly sure that the environmental arguments had been grossly exaggerated, that the aeroplane was hardly likely to be unsafe if it had been certified in Britain and France, and if it was being flown by two of the world's leading airlines. It was interesting that they should have taken so long to come out. It seemed almost as if they were afraid of being shouted down. Perhaps they thought that by then all the 'antis' had gone to bed . . .

Attempts to overturn Secretary Coleman's decision ended in the Supreme Court when Chief Justice Warren E. Burger refused any further appeals with the single word: 'Denied.'

At 12 degrees west, on 24 May 1976, this time in Alpha Charlie, we heard from Pierre Dudal that his flight, Air France 053, was nicely tucked in behind. Both take-offs had been to the west, and the timing had turned out to be accurate. It was a beautiful day, the weather at Dulles was forecast fine, and the passengers were having a marvellous time. There was filming, of course, interviewing, picture-taking in front of the Machmeters, but it was all a good deal more orderly than the inaugural to Bahrain had been. No one wore fancy dress.

In addition to 31 fare-paying passengers, there were a couple of dozen journalists and a group of airline guests from politics and industry. This time I was in the left-hand seat and Norman Todd was the co-pilot – he would command the return flight. Behind us was our most senior flight engineer, Lou Bolton, who, coming from the 747 flight and therefore accustomed to masses of space, had made the definitive observation on the size of Concorde's toilets:

'You need to make up your mind what you're going to do before you go in,' he claimed, a little unfairly.

The descent, including the first 'fall off the wall' went perfectly. AF053 was now close behind. Almost as soon as we entered the Dulles area we were slowed down to our minimum speed – not a very good omen, but we didn't argue, as the controller's voice had some notes of tension in it. We discovered why later.

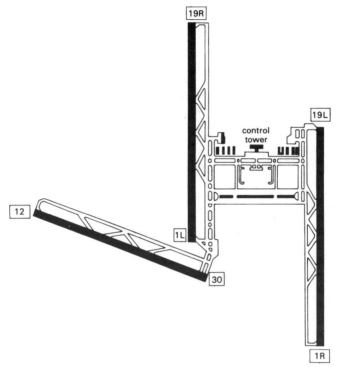

Dulles Airport

We were to land on runway 01 Right – the northerly runway on the eastern side of the airfield. As we started the 'downwind leg' – parallel, flying south – the controller warned us that there was a light aircraft ahead, not responding to instructions to leave. We saw it immediately – a single-engined, high-wing monoplane. No evasive action was needed since he was moving gently out of the way. We passed him, to our left and a few hundred feet above, and carried on to the landing. Dudal followed, landing two minutes later. We taxied by different routes – all worked out beforehand – so as to arrive from opposite directions in front of the control tower. Difficult to judge, that was.

The aircraft, rolling towards each other with their long noses stretching out ahead, seemed eager to meet.

The two marshallers sensibly stayed on either side of the painted centreline in order to avoid a collision as they walked backwards. We stopped, rather suddenly, at the same time. In a final gesture, to seal the joint arrival, we raised the two noses and visors together.

Dudal and I were to present our flight plans to a representative of the Smithsonian Institute and to attend a press conference, so we each left for the terminal with our passengers. I had never seen anything like the scene in the room set aside for the conference. At the centre of a long table on a platform sat Sir Edmund Dell, the British Secretary of State for Trade, and Marcel Cavaillé, the French Minister of Transportation. On either side of them were ranged other senior figures. Pierre Dudal and I were at opposite ends.

In front of the table was the most alarming crush of broadcasters, reporters and cameramen, who struggled for position and occasionally fought. Unfortunately, as soon as the introductory speeches were over, they all seemed to head for me. The encounter with the light aircraft was what interested them. I found myself surrounded by questioning faces and microphones. It seemed to go on forever.

Not quite forever. We finally escaped to our hotel in Washington, where I was at last able to telephone the control tower for the full story. They explained the tension in the controller's voice. Shortly before our arrival, light aircraft had begun to converge on Dulles from every direction. In their own words, 'the edges of the scopes went green'. The tower put into effect an emergency procedure which allows them to order all uncontrolled aircraft away from the vicinity of an airfield. All but one had responded. Most of them had probably just come to see the fun, but what about the one that stayed?

The *Houston Post* reported the next day: 'The aircraft might have been a photo plane trying to take pictures of the 1400-mile-per-hour Concorde.' The *Washington Star* had a little more to say: 'The identity of the plane was not immediately available. Photographers from the *Star* were in the air in a single-engine plane at the time to photograph the arrivals.'

Controversy surrounded our departure, too. We took off,

according to some newspapers, on the wrong runway. We cheated. We evaded the noise monitors ... The Air France return flight had taken off before we started our aircraft checks. He had used runway 19 Left – the same one we had landed on the previous day, but in the opposite direction. We chose to use 19 Right – a choice which any airman is allowed to make. The FAA knew that we would use this runway as often as possible, simply because its departure route took us over fewer communities. That, after all, is one of the best ways of minimizing the effect of aircraft noise. Using it would mean that we would have to accept occasional delays, as other aircraft landed, but we were prepared to accept that disadvantage.

As we tuned the radios in, it became clear that the frequency was being used by someone other than the controllers and the aircraft – someone who sounded as if he was connected with the noise monitoring (but didn't trouble to identify himself) and who had presumably persuaded the Air France captain to use 19 Left, where the monitoring equipment had been placed. When we asked for 19 Right for take-off, he shouted, 'They can't do that!' The tower, however, granted our request, entirely in accordance with the rules, so we took off, leaving some very angry officials behind. Not in the tower – up to the waist in poison ivy off the end of the other runway. Secretary Coleman was embarrassed and issued a public rebuke. I take this opportunity to apologize. No harm was meant – we were simply doing our best.

In spite of the predictable number of irrelevant stories about near-misses and cheating the monitors, the flights received, in general, a good press. Everything had happened according to schedule, the 'white birds' were lovely to look at, not half as frightening as they had been pictured. The public – the people who really mattered – would now be able to judge for themselves. A woman who lived near the airport, interviewed by a Washington paper, said: 'You know what I think? All this about the Concorde is silly.'

11.   . . . and New York

Soon after the Coleman decision, while plans for the first Washington flights were being made, it was announced that Air France and British Airways intended to start services to New York on 10 April. This was a finesse, designed to make the Port Authority take some action which could be challenged at law. The Authority responded quickly, with a ban on Concorde flights to JFK until at least six months of evaluation had been completed at Dulles. Their spokesman explained that the ban had been imposed solely on the grounds of noise and the Port Authority's liability to damage suits. He added that the legality of the ban would have to be tested in the courts – a clear enough hint to the other side.

The airlines announced they would file a suit against the Port, but were curiously slow about doing so. The reason was that there was a growing difference of opinion between the two national groups pressing for Concorde's entry. The French government and Aerospatiale had for some time employed several public relations and lobbying organizations to advise them. The advice – and it came from, among others, an ex-Senator, Charles Goodell, and an ex-Deputy Mayor of New York, Richard Aurelio – was that it would be imprudent to take court action until all other means had been tried. The legal process could produce the wrong result, and, once started, was irreversible. The American public, they felt, would eventually come round if the case was well-explained, and then the politicians would follow.

The British, and in particular British Airways, who were advised only by their US counsel, William Clarke, were quite sure that the Port (backed by the State Governor) would resist any Federal pressure, and that the ban, which they believed was totally illegal, was bound to be overturned in court.

There was another, temporary factor. 1976 was a Presidential election year. In his campaign, Jimmy Carter made his opposition clear. President Ford was thought to be more sympathetic, but during the run-up to the election it was unlikely that there would be any unpopular exercise of Federal power. In this atmosphere of uncertainty, political initiatives were stalled. And the two groups couldn't agree to go to court.

As the summer passed, demand for the flights to Washington was high. Average load factors of well over 80 per cent began to make the point that passengers were by-passing New York. There were further, unsuccessful court actions to overturn the Coleman decision. In September, the Administrator of the FAA said that his agency would support the airlines' litigation, if necessary. The airlines replied that the action would begin in January.

But it didn't. The delay was perhaps caused by a desire to wait for some sign of the new Administration's attitude. Both Prime Minister Callaghan and President Giscard d'Estaing made direct appeals to President Carter soon after his inauguration. Then, in February 1977, the President let it be known that he re-affirmed the Coleman ruling, but that he could not force the Port Authority to let Concorde in. The Port, meanwhile, was putting off any permanent decision as long as it could. Meetings to review the ban were called and postponed. It was claimed that there was not enough evidence yet. They warned again of damage suits. This could go on for ever.

On 4 March, Goodell arranged a meeting with the Port Authority. He promised them that at the meeting the airlines and manufacturers would present new evidence that they could meet JFK's noise standards. The meeting was arranged for 9 March – the day before the Port's next review of the ban. Goodell's assumption was that, by the offer of what might be seen as concessions, they could be made to change their minds. He had made the arrangement without consulting British Airways, who were horrified by the whole business – they had always wanted to go to court and get the ban overturned, and then show, in actual service, that the standards would be met.

This initiative by France's adviser led to some acrimonious discussions between the two national groups, who held such different views on how to achieve the same end, but it did, finally, produce a resolution of their disagreements. The meeting took place as scheduled, and the Port was given an outline of the proposals. A further, more detailed presentation was arranged for 1 April. The French and British agreed that if this did not produce the required result they would go to court on the 28th.

Behind the offer of the so-called concessions was the fact that two of the manufacturers' most talented engineers had been working out a detailed analysis of just how our operations at Kennedy would work, over a whole year. Henri Perrier of Aerospatiale and Bob McKinlay of BAC were in the process of putting together the results, in what came to be known by us as the 'grey book'.

Ever since the end of the route-proving, the manufacturers and the two airlines had been working together on flying techniques to reduce community noise. Early on, a general procedure had been arrived at. It had been refined for the particular needs of each of Heathrow's and Dulles's runways. After that it was a question of applying it to JFK.

The airport is nearly surrounded by communities which creep

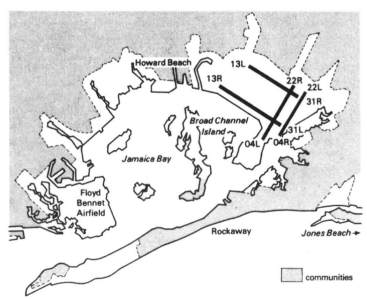

Kennedy Airport and its environs

right up to its boundaries, particularly in the semi-circle from the north-west to the south-east. On the other, south-westerly side, however, lies Jamaica Bay. Noise routes for subsonic aircraft already made use of the bay as a gap through which they could fly, away from populated areas. Obviously this was a help. So, too, was the fact that any aircraft leaving Kennedy for Europe would soon be out over the sea, for that is where the airways lie.

We could make good use of some features of the aircraft, as well. Its excellent handling qualities meant that we were able to fly a rather tighter pattern than most aircraft around the bay. This was especially useful on departures from runway 31 Left. It would keep us away from the township of Howard Beach, which had grown in recent years to a point very close to the end of the runways. The residents there were particularly exposed to aircraft noise, and vociferous in their opposition to Concorde which, they were led to believe, would add to their problems.

The take-off to the north-east (runway 04 Left) was the worst – no manoeuvre would help. On this route, until the aircraft was over the sea it was bound to be flying over people – large numbers of them. Its use should be avoided entirely, if possible, and Concorde's performance helped here. Because it is unusually good at taking off in crosswinds and tailwinds, we would be able to use other runways.

Finally, on all take-offs, our weight would be a good deal less than the maximum – the route from New York to London is well inside the aircraft's range, and nothing like the full fuel capacity would be needed.

Perrier's and McKinlay's analysis of New York weather, and the statistics of runway usage, showed that we would be able to use runways 31 Left and 22 Right most of the time, with only a tiny proportion leaving from 13 Right. It showed that all take-offs would be within JFK's noise criteria and that each would produce a pattern very like that of a Boeing 707-320B. It proved that our average take-off weight would be some 14 tons below the maximum and that, when our operations were added to all the others at the airfield, there would be no noticeable difference to the communities' total exposure to noise.

These conclusions were set out, runway by runway, in the 'grey book'. It took the combined resources of the manufacturers and the airlines several months to produce what was probably the most thoroughly researched study of aircraft noise impact ever made. The book's correctness couldn't be argued about – it was too scholarly for that. It is worth mentioning, to show how complex the task was, that several pages were devoted purely to the definition of terms, and that it worked out an accurate way of compensating for the fact that the Port used its own special units of noise measurement (called, by them, PNdB but, on average, reading about two units higher than the international standard).

The 'grey book' was presented to the Port Authority on 1 April by a team which included Dudal and myself. They were obviously impressed. We left the meeting satisfied that we had done all we could to get the facts straight, and to allow the Port's executives to grasp the nettle of approval if they felt inclined. They retired for a period of meditation on the proposals.

It was obvious that matters were coming to a head: that either the Port would now remove their ban or the court would decide, on the 28th. During the intervening weeks the protest groups became feverishly active. Local meetings and demonstrations were held in most of the suburbs around Kennedy. A motorcade, designed to block the approach roads to the airport, took place on 17 April, in spite of a court injunction banning it. But only 600-odd cars turned out, against the expected 2000 to 4000.

The results of a Gallup poll on Concorde were published: 75 per cent of those interviewed had heard of the issue – a remarkably high proportion; 43 per cent believed Concorde should be allowed to land in the US, and 39 per cent believed it shouldn't. When asked whether it should be allowed 'to land at the major airport nearest here', the figures were slightly more than reversed. It was an answer typical of the attitudes of most of us to difficult questions about the siting of airports, missiles or nuclear power stations – we may approve of them in principle, but only so long as they're somewhere else.

What none of them knew, for no one believed it (or was prepared to say so), was that there was no real problem. The information was locked away in the Port Authority's offices at the towering World Trade Centre buildings in lower Manhattan. Their answer had not come by the 28th, so the court hearing finally took place, before Judge Milton Pollack. Early in the proceedings he criticized the Port for having taken so long to reach a decision. He asked them to explain 'how anyone can have a fair trial without a test landing'.

On 11 May, Judge Pollack overturned the ban. The Port immediately lodged an appeal. The appeal judge allowed the ban to stay, temporarily, while it asked for briefs from the French and British governments, the Department of Transportation, and the State Department. On 14 June the appeal judges upheld the ban, but pointed out that it was only sustainable if it was 'fair, reasonable and non-discriminatory'. This question was referred back to the lower court. The case returned to Judge Pollack who declared the ban illegal on the grounds that it was indeed unreasonable, because of the Port's 'excessive and unjustified' delays.

A second appeal was rejected. Chief Judge Irving R. Kaufman summed up the story nicely: 'I cannot help but have the feeling that the Port Authority does not want to come to grips with this thing.' The battle moved to the Supreme Court, the final arbiter of all matters legal and constitutional. On 17 October 1977 the Court finally declared in Concorde's favour.

So, in the end, the legal process turned out to be the answer. It is hard to guess just how much the Port's vacillations helped to make up the judges' minds. However, it is certain that throughout the hearings and appeals the Port was never able to prove that it had made any serious attempt to find solid grounds for its ban.

After the Supreme Court's judgment, British Airways and Air France promptly announced that the aeroplane would arrive two days later, to carry out proving flights. The FAA planned to put up extra noise-monitoring stations around the airport, in addition to the four fixed posts already there. Local opponents turned their wrath on the Port Authority – it should have produced new noise regulations, which, they believed, would have barred Concorde without the now-illegal ban. (The Port's difficulty here was that such regulations would have barred most of the other aircraft, too.) They planned further lawsuits. New York State's Governor Carey, however, declared that he would 'uphold the rule of law'.

The long delay in clearing the path to New York must have cost the manufacturers and airlines incalculable sums, but in technical terms it had some benefit. Two of JFK's runways had long been known to have corrugations in them which made subsonic take-offs rough, and might just possibly produce the old problem of 'nose nodding' in Concorde. Measurements were taken from other aircraft, but they were not easily transferable – they were affected by the behaviour of the aeroplanes in which the instruments were carried. In a normal world we would simply have taken an aircraft to the runways and tested them, but Concorde's world was never normal. After all, not long ago a debate on a Long Island radio programme had produced the amazing suggestion that Concorde had caused the cold winter of 1976/7, and the latest fashion among protesters was to claim that its fuel tanks would blow up. Even mentioning the subject of runway response would have brought forth cries of 'Danger!'

So the proving flights would include an assessment of the runways – in particular the worst one, 31 Left. Fortunately the undercarriage manufacturer had, earlier in the year, come up with the modification we had been asking for – the two-stage hydraulic damper. The aircraft were fitted with it during the summer. The proving flights would be needed in any case, to check the accuracy of the noise procedures, but some of the sting had been taken out of the runway problem.

Aircraft 201 – F-WTSB – left Toulouse for New York on 19 October. Jean Franchi, Aerospatiale's Chief Test Pilot, was in command. A small, precise Corsican, his somewhat dour expression was relieved by a distinct twinkle in the eye. He was going to enjoy this. The airlines' captains were on board: Pierre Dudal for Air France in the co-pilot's seat, Brian Walpole and Tony Meadows representing British Airways. Gordon Corps, Chief Test Pilot of the CAA's Airworthiness Division, was there, too. In the cabin were all the technicians who would analyse the data and maintain the aeroplane. Franchi's relaxed geniality set the mood – he had no doubts whatsoever of the outcome.

No one knew what the reception would be like, except that it was a pretty fair guess that a large number of protesters would turn out, and that the press would be there in force, waiting to make the instant judgments they thought their readers wanted. The flight was cleared to land on runway 04 Left – a happy chance for the first arrival, as its approach is over Jamaica Bay. Lining up with the runway, still out over the sea, the crew were met with an astonishing sight – a row of helicopters on each side of the approach path: ten or a dozen, stepped down all the way to the runway. Franchi pointed his machine down this aerial staircase and called the tower, asking piously whether the noise monitors were in position. They were, of course. As the aircraft passed by, a reading of 105·5 PNdB was recorded (including, perhaps, the helicopters) – for the protesters, depressingly low.

After touchdown, Sierra Bravo rolled to a stop on a runway lined on either side by people. There were even more along the edges of the taxiway. Presumably every airport worker who had a pass had come in to watch the arrival. Some raised their thumbs, some turned them down. There were a few clenched fists. As the aircraft taxied on, the numbers of watchers increased until in places they stood four or five deep. By now most of them were giving signs of approval. On arrival at the maintenance area – where, for security reasons, the aircraft was to be parked – those on board learned for the first time how successful the arrival had been.

Over 500 press men and women assembled in a hangar to interview the crew. Many of them were from local Queens, Brooklyn and Long Island papers which had run campaigns against Concorde. Their questions were not exactly hostile, but they were undoubtedly probing, with an edge. Franchi fielded them with a certain panache. The story of the undercarriage had got out. One reporter asked how he had found the runway.

'It is a runway. It is concrete.'

The aeroplane hadn't been as noisy as expected. Had he done anything different for New York?

'Why should I do anything different in New York from what I do in Toulouse? They are my friends there!'

The session was suddenly interrupted by a loud clanking – the hangar doors were being rolled back. The noise made further talk impossible, and all heads turned as 201 was towed into a space behind the crew. The doors were shut and the questions continued, but in a subtly different way. They were no less searching, but somehow the presence of the actual aircraft they were being asked about altered the tone of voice. Sitting there, demure and blameless, she demanded a certain respect.

The next day saw the first take-off. Brian Walpole was in the captain's seat, with Franchi alongside as co-pilot. In case anyone thought that the flights were being used as a demonstration by test pilots, employing some trick techniques, this first departure was being done by an airline pilot. Walpole, lined up on 31 Left and ready to go, was acutely aware of how much depended on the next few minutes. He tightened his straps against the possibility of disturbance from the runway, and silently rehearsed the departure procedure. This was the one involving a 25-degree banked turn soon after lift-off, taking the aircraft around the edge of the bay, with a power cut-back just before passing Howard Beach. The opposition had, of course, claimed that it was dangerous, and hoped it wouldn't work anyway.

He had practised this take-off many times in the simulator, with every conceivable failure and in every possible condition of wind and temperature, but this was for real. If ever he had to get it right, it was now. He set off down the runway with full power. The afterburners lit up. The aircraft reached the intersection where the roughness was expected, and – nothing, or very little. Good. V_1 – rotate – gear up – 100 feet – roll 25 degrees of bank on, and there it is. Nicely settled in the turn.

On the side of the runway a large number of faces were tilted upwards, following his progress. Tony Meadows had gone out with the reporters to watch the take-off. He was worried, because 31 Left was not the runway in use that morning by all the other departures – so Concorde would be taking off on its own. Anyone who has stood close to a runway as an aircraft takes off knows that it is quite a noisy affair. His concern was that many of the reporters would be experiencing their first close-up take-off, with no comparison from other aircraft by which to judge it.

Fortunately, the runway-in-use was changed to 31 Left just before departure time, and aircraft began to take off from it before Concorde taxied out. The first was a 707. Its pilot, having perhaps heard of the famous Concorde turn, and seeing the assembled watchers, started his bank rather earlier than usual. A 747 followed. This aircraft tried to go one better – it nearly put its left-hand wheels back on the runway and, as a result, went a little uncertainly into the turn. Then Concorde took off. It was not much noisier – they'd all been pretty shattering at this range – but the turn appeared to start later than the 747's, and the bank angle, presumably because of its much smaller wing span, looked less. It all seemed much calmer. One of the TV people standing nearby said, disappointed: 'It's a non-event.'

Immediately afterwards, another aircraft took off. It went straight ahead some way before banking. A bystander commented: 'Look at the bum. He's not turning.' The message was beginning to get through.

The turn was, in fact, a perfectly normal procedure. The departure instructions, which applied to all aircraft, said that after take-off the pilot should 'turn as soon as feasible' – it was just a question of where and how it was done. Those subsonic aircraft had shown graphically that an early turn helped the residents at Howard Beach, and that Concorde could execute it more neatly than the others. Proof lay in what they had seen for themselves, at last, and in the Authority's monitor. Set to record only at a level of 105 (Port) PNdB or more, it wasn't even triggered. The noise limit was 112.

The flight went out into the Atlantic, beyond Gander, then returned to New York. On landing, the noise measurements were again very low – less than the values recorded from several aircraft arriving before and after. The crew had no idea of how successful the flight had been until they arrived back at the hangar, where Bob McKinlay's broad grin and upraised thumb gave them the answer. The next day, Pierre Dudal repeated the exercise, leaving the noise monitor's recorder undisturbed again. On the 22nd, 201 went back home to Toulouse.

During the month's gap between 201's return and the inaugural airline services, the opposition collapsed. After a few ritual threats, the specially created groups began to disband. They claimed, however, probably quite justifiably, that although they had lost on Concorde, they had won on noise – the whole subject had been raised to a new level of political importance. The *New York Times* reported that the residents of Howard Beach, who had become famous for their opposition to Concorde, resented having been 'made to look stupid', since the aeroplane wasn't noticeably noisier and the value of their homes hadn't dropped.

For the crew and technicians on board 201, for the airlines, for the manufacturers and for the two governments, it was the end of a long, exhausting struggle. Until Concorde actually arrived at New York, there was always a strong possibility that she would never be allowed to go there: having been, and come back, she had won her right to the route for which she had been designed. There was never a final battle – only anti-climax when the enemy withdrew from the field.

On 22 November 1977, Dudal and Walpole took the first airline services to New York. Leaving Heathrow, Brian Walpole had arrived at the runway twenty minutes early. He apologized to the passengers for the delay, and hoped they would forgive it – after all, it wasn't much, compared with the twenty months it had taken to get to this point.

Once more, the two aircraft flew across the Atlantic in tandem, this time with the Air France aircraft in front, and made the now-traditional joint arrival. After landing, they posed briefly together for the photographers, then taxied to their own terminals. There was no press conference, only some casual interviews. The New York Chamber of Commerce provided a banquet luncheon for around a thousand people, to celebrate their city's entrance into the supersonic age.

New York proved, as expected, to be Concorde's market. On average, the flights are 80 per cent full, and most of the passengers are regulars. As far as noise is concerned, both airlines have performed, over the years, slightly better than the 'grey book' promised they would. On Jones Beach, in the summer, groups of people stand up and shield their eyes against the sun, sometimes wave, as Concorde turns out over the sea and points her nose towards Nantucket.

12. Impressions

By now, I suppose, it must be obvious that I care for Concorde rather more than a man might normally be expected to care about a machine. She has occupied a place in my life rather like a child's. Beautiful and demanding, talented and difficult, she entered my life stealthily, and then proceeded, as a child does, to take part of it over. She required and deserved loyalty. She needed civilizing, and preparing for a harsh adult world. She had to be defended, too.

I don't claim to be impartial, although I have tried to understand her opponents' points of view. Rather, as a parent feels for a child's crises and setbacks, so I have felt hers as if they were my own. Criticisms, particularly if they are unfair, hurt. Triumphs are matters for family rejoicing. She was certainly fit and healthy when – grown up, as it were – she went out into the world as an airliner.

But, even then, her path wasn't strewn with roses. After passing the hardest and most important test of them all – entry into New York – her routes were extended, first to Singapore and then to Dallas, Texas. For a time she was flown by the Texan pilots of Braniff Airlines, and the *sarong kebayas* of Singapore Airlines' stewardesses once more graced her cabin. Sadly, neither route survived the massive increase in fuel costs and the worldwide recession of the late 1970s. Both were closed down in 1980.

A tragedy, we all felt. She might have gone on from Singapore to Tokyo or Australia. She still might, one day. But, if you fly Concorde, you get used to setbacks and learn to concentrate on the possible. The routes to North and South America, and in particular to New York, are her prime ones, and here she finds her market. She positively eats the journey across the Atlantic, and we have all adapted – her passengers included – to the new time-frame her speed creates.

As far as flying can ever be, it's routine now. Sometimes it is hard to remember what it felt like in the early days. But such intense associations, such battles fought together, leave indelible impressions – of the flights, of the people Concorde serves, of the bitterness that once surrounded her, and of the pleasure we all take in her performance.

'It is absolutely abhorrent to us. We won't tolerate it. Scratch it and rip it out!' Bryan Levinson, leader of a group called Concorde Alert, and of a civic association at Howard Beach, New York, reported in the *Philadelphia Inquirer*, 18 October 1977.

'I had fears like everyone else. I've had planes at four in the morning, wide open. I thought they were going to hit the house. And this Concorde came by – sleep.' Unidentified resident of the Jamaica Bay area, New York, interviewed by WCBS-TV, 21 October 1977.

The London morning papers arrive at Kennedy Airport on the early morning flight. They are set out in the Concorde lounge at the British Airways terminal for passengers to read as they sit with croissants or canapés, coffee or champagne, overlooking the needle nose parked only a few feet away. Telephones are available for last-minute calls, and there is an air of quiet comfort. With the minimum of fuss, it is made clear that the special needs of people who travel a great deal, and who have paid extra for their Concorde flight, will be attended to properly.

There are usually some families – even, occasionally, small children. Some of the passengers are elderly. They may have felt that flying by Concorde, perhaps on just one leg of their journey, is an attractive way of celebrating a golden wedding. But most have done it before. Fred Finn, whose job takes him around the world for most of each year, clocked up his millionth Concorde mile in June 1980 – over 270 flights in four years, more than one a week. He uses Concorde, he says, because it helps to preserve his health from the effects of his crippling travel schedule, because it saves time, because he feels better at the end of a flight, and because he likes the friendly, clubby atmosphere. He also likes what he calls the 'sports-car feeling' of the aeroplane, and the fact that, as one of only a hundred passengers, he doesn't have to wait long for his baggage. He knows all the crews; they know his likes and dislikes. He feels at home.

Interviewer: 'Your dog is affected by the Concorde?'
Man: 'Oh, yes.'
Interviewer: 'How so?'
Man: 'He starts howling, he gets frightened. You'd be surprised how noisy it is.'
Interviewer: 'Well, what's your name, sir?'
Man: 'I . . .'
Interviewer: 'What's the name of your dog, sir?'
Man: 'Beau. Beau Brummel.'
Interviewer: 'Beau Brummel?'
Man: 'That's right.'

WCBS-TV, 21 October 1977

I like to meet the passengers when I can and, since that is not easy to do on the short flight – during most of which the drink and meal trolleys are out in the aisles – I often visit them in the lounge before departure. This gives me a clearer idea of whom I shall be talking to as I keep them informed of the progress of the flight, and lets them see who is going to fly them.

On the rare occasion when there is any substantial delay I tell them about it, face to face. I tell them, as simply but as exactly as possible, what the trouble is. Almost invariably the passengers take bad news about delays philosophically, and appreciate frankness. Generally, their reaction is: 'Fine, Captain. You tell us when you are ready, and we'll come along.'

But this kind of approach can have its penalties. One day, just before leaving New York, there was a sudden fall of snow followed by an equally sudden rise in air temperature – to just above freezing point – which turned the inch-deep layer into a glutinous mixture resembling nothing more than lemon sorbet. I drove out in a car to poke and prod it on the runway, and returned, damp-footed, to tell the passengers we would have to wait. The conversation went something like this:

'Ladies and gentlemen, you can see that there's snow on the

runways. I'm afraid it's turned to slush, and we'll have to wait for it to melt. If the temperature stays up, we should be able to go in –'

'He's lying,' a woman standing next to me interjected.

'. . . about an hour. Slush affects the take-off performance of all aircraft . . .'

'He's not going, you know. He just wants to keep us here so we won't go with another airline.'

'Concorde "could melt ice caps", says Mr Wiggs.' Daily Mail, 11 February 1969.

'CONCORDE "CAUSES TORNADOS".' Slough and Hounslow Evening Mail, 31 July 1974.

Pat Allen, our only Australian captain, had a rather better reception on another occasion. In the early days of flights to Washington, before a series of modifications had improved the aeroplane's capacity, we were somewhat restricted, having to balance payload against range. A full load of passengers checked in for his flight, before he discovered that the combination of severe headwinds and high temperatures simply didn't permit him to carry all of them, plus adequate fuel reserves. He went to see them, set out the problem, and offered them a choice: either some would have to stay behind, or, if they preferred, all the bags could be taken off and sent over on a following subsonic flight. Unanimously, cheering Pat's openness, they opted to go without the bags.

'. . . There isn't a chance approaching that of an icicle in hell that the Concorde will ever be allowed to touch down in American airports.' Professor John Kenneth Galbraith, in a letter to the London *Times*, 5 April 1971.

Many flights stand out in the memory. So do some of the passengers. Mohammed Ali, cradling his tiny daughter, seemed astonishingly mild, and wrote us what he described as 'the world's fastest poem'. Carol Channing filled Concorde with her charm. But my favourite of all is a very old Englishwoman who decided she wanted to make the round trip to America in a day

– just for fun. When she appeared, very frail and obviously excited, the staff in the lounge began to worry about whether she was fit enough for the journey, and tried gently to dissuade her. However, she was made of tougher stuff than they guessed. As she approached the door, I heard her ask, a little testily, what the young man who was holding her arm really thought might happen.

'Well, madam . . . well, the excitement might, er . . . well, er . . . kill you.'

One of her two sticks waved as her voice boomed the reply:

'What a lovely way to go, young man!'

'You usually go over our house and can be seen from the kitchen, but when they call "Here is Concorde!" by the time I get there you are gone, over Richmond Park. I have arthritis, and of course it's a nuisance. Anyway, please come in like you did today and I will see you. A bit nearer the river.' Letter, 1976.

The cabin crew do a spectacular job, performing a sort of aerial ballet as they produce drinks and meals for their passengers, working with discreet precision, but always having time, somehow, to stop and chat.

British air cabin crew have become legendary on the great international routes. They have a well-deserved reputation for efficiency, warmth and a brand of unflappable humour which survives every crisis. A nice illustration happened years ago on a Comet, when, after landing, the captain put the brakes on rather sharply. The chief steward, who had been – quite improperly – standing at the back of the cabin, lost his balance and shot down the aisle on his back. He ended up in the first-class cabin, alongside a surprised passenger, of whom he enquired:

'You rang, sir?'

Nobody stands up in the back of Concorde's cabin, but the spirit is unchanged. It's a closely knit team, from the captain right through to the steward or stewardess working in the rear galley. Discipline, in the formal sense, hardly ever needs to be imposed – it's there from the nature of the jobs and the people who do them. The result is a *camaraderie* which makes flying the aeroplane a special pleasure for all of us.

'I am one of your passengers from Japan ... and enjoyed your kind service and a pleasant trip.

'Then I had a favour of you to ask that you should send Technical Documents to my son who have major in aeromechanics in University of Tokyo ... My son are very glad to thank you. I say too thank you for your kindness ... May you have a happier life.' Letter, 1979.

Some of us, chiefly around the times of the inaugural flights, found ourselves in the news. It was an enlightening experience for me, and it had its pleasant features. I heard from a large number of old friends with whom I had lost touch, invitations arrived for all sorts of parties, doors opened everywhere. It was easy to see why people like being famous, and how swiftly and completely the machinery of the media can create fame. But, despite the fact that we were protected by a very capable press department, who gave reporters the information they needed, and, where possible, arranged appointments, I wondered how anybody could stand the constant intrusions on privacy that newsworthiness, even if temporary, brings.

My house, my family, my bicycle – with me on it – were photographed. I baulked at having my breakfast filmed before going to Washington ('Condemned man eats...'), but gave in over playing cricket – and was promptly bowled out, first ball. One photographer wanted a picture of me fishing. When I explained that I hadn't fished for years, he replied: 'That doesn't matter. Where's the nearest river? We'll buy a rod on the way.'

On inaugural day at New York. 'Those present were treated to:

"A series of small but vituperative arguments between cameramen and people who stepped in front of their lenses ...

"The sight of a passenger almost ripped limb from limb after he gave extensive interviews to a gaggle of reporters at the exit from US Customs, then admitted that he too was a reporter ...

"The spectacle of a television crew trying to convince a cabbie to pose as an anti-Concorde demonstrator outside the British Airways terminal.

"You're against it, aren't you?" one of the crew demanded.

"Well, yeah, I guess," the cabbie said.

Impressions 227

"Well, then," said the television man, as if the matter was decided.'

Philadelphia Inquirer, 23 November 1977.

Perhaps the most fascinating aspect of the press view of Concorde was the way it consistently failed to sense the underlying mood of the public. Just after the publication of the GLC report, a crew from a New York radio station arrived to sample the views of people around Heathrow. They wanted to record the aircraft's noise and to interview some local people directly under the departure path, so I took them to a site, which we chose together, just west of the aiport. We pulled in on some space in front of a small group of shops, and the radio crews unpacked their equipment. A shopowner came out to see what was going on. When he found out, he went back to get his wife, and together they gave the reporter a very thorough lecture on the good behaviour of Concorde and the wickedness of the New Yorkers who were keeping her out.

The crew, a little shaken by being held personally responsible for the New York delay, measured the noise as Concorde passed overhead, and that didn't show anything unusual. Customers of the shops (one in carpet slippers) arrived, eager to have their say. The man wearing the slippers, I remember, gave them a particularly hard time. I was almost as astonished as the crew, because these people lived in a very noisy place, and Concorde certainly wasn't making it any quieter. What I could detect, though, was pride, both in the achievement which Concorde represented, and in its extraordinary beauty. They mentioned this several times.

'This is a sad day for our people, to realize the Government has betrayed them like this.' Carol Berman, leader of the Emergency Coalition to Stop the SST, later elected to the New York State Senate.

'It was no noisier than other planes. It could be we've all been had by a little demagoguery for political careers.' A resident of Long Island.

Both quotes from the *Long Island Newsday*, 23 November 1977.

The depth of public feeling really began to come home to me when, in 1978, my local pub decided it would like to hire Concorde for its annual outing. Its proprietor, Ian Macaulay, is principally a farmer, and looks the part. He is a straightforward eccentric, if that is possible – large, bluff and full of original ideas for entertaining his customers. So I passed on his request, and a few months later the answer came back (rather to my surprise) that it could be done. Within a week, before Ian had got around to putting a notice up, he had 170 applicants for the 100 seats.

And so, in September, the Bell Inn went supersonic, around the Bay of Biscay. The two-and-a-half-hour flight carried a marvellous mixture of people – surgeons and tractor drivers, landowners and gamekeepers, grandmothers and young children. I flew them on their journey. It was, I think, the most purely happy flight I have ever done. Their enthusiasm was irresistible.

Although we had tried to keep the plans secret, the news got out several days beforehand. First the local, then the national, then the world's press zoomed in on the Bell. The whole idea seemed to them astonishing – this was an 'elitist' aeroplane, only for the privileged few, for diplomats, film stars, company presidents. Who were these people?

The reporters came to the Bell (one interview took place alongside a dung-heap: it was muck-spreading time), and they found out. In the process they began at last to uncover what people really felt – people who hadn't said much, but who had their own views. My only regret was that it took them so long.

'She flies over this house twice a day, and it always gives me such a thrill to hear her. If it is clear enough I always have to dash out to watch her, and I never get tired of seeing such a beautiful aircraft.' Letter, 1978.

'Assemblywoman Gerdi E. Lipschutz . . . suggested that angry residents fly kites to clog the middle of the landing approaches to Kennedy.' UPI report in the Peekskill, New York, *Evening Star*, 18 October 1977.

'*Dear Captains of Concorde, Thank you in your very busy world for the lovely photographs of Concorde. My husband and I enjoyed them to the full, looking at them through a magnifying glass.*' Letter, 1979.

In the end, it is not the bad feelings – the hysteria, the distortions, the political manoeuvres – that have endured, but the good ones: people, places, sights and sounds. Passengers unfolding their newspapers as we start the engines. Accelerating down the runway like a racehorse from a starting gate. The view through the visor of the earth rotating slowly ten miles below. The sun rising in the west. The pterodactyl approach.

I wake up happy on a day when I am going to fly, and I thank God for the series of coincidences which brought me here, first into aviation and then to Concorde. There are many grander, more important careers, but none that can be as much fun as mine.

I, and my friends, fly Concorde. Not *a* Concorde, not *the* Concorde, nor *Concordes*. She's the only aeroplane I know that is always referred to by her name.

Postscript

Since 1976, when she entered service, and even since 1981, when this book was written, the world's view of Concorde has changed utterly. Scheduled flights at Mach 2 are now normal, and a large number of people for whom time is vital use her almost like a commuter train. Many of those who can't afford to cross the Atlantic in Concorde have experienced the excitement of supersonic flight on charters — to such an extent that these flights have become an important part of Concorde's revenue.

The Press is now almost wholly in favour, and British Airways is so confident of Concorde's public reception that it uses her to promote subsonic routes and to advertise the airline's presence in new areas. Cities that previously banned Concorde now invite her to special celebrations.

Concorde has truly come of age.

Brian Calvert
1988

The Aircraft

Type	Registration No.		First flight	From	Place & date of retirement		Delivery date	
Prototype	F-WTSS	001	2.3.69	Toulouse	Le Bourget	19.10.73		
Prototype	G-BSST	002	9.4.69	Filton	Yeovilton	4.3.76		
Pre-production	G-AXDN	01	17.12.71	Filton	Duxford	20.8.77		
Pre-production	F-WTSA	02	10.1.73	Toulouse	Orly	20.5.76		
Production[1]	F-WTSB	201	6.12.73	Toulouse				
Production[1]	G-BBDG	202	13.2.74	Filton	Filton	1981		
Production	F-WTSC[2]	203	31.1.75	Toulouse			6.1.76	(AF)[7]
Production	G-BOAC	204	27.2.75	Filton			13.2.76	(BA)
Production	F-BVFA	205	25.10.75	Toulouse			19.12.75	(AF)
Production	G-BOAA	206	5.11.75	Filton			14.1.76	(BA)
Production	F-BVFB	207	6.3.76	Toulouse			8.4.76	(AF)
Production	G-BOAB	208	18.5.76	Filton			30.9.76	(BA)
Production	F-BVFC	209	9.7.76	Toulouse			27.7.76	(AF)
Production	G-BOAD	210	25.8.76	Filton			6.12.76	(BA)
Production	F-BVFD	211	10.2.77	Toulouse			26.3.77	(AF)
Production	G-BOAE	212	17.3.77	Filton			20.7.77	(BA)
Production	F-WJAM[3]	213	26.6.78	Toulouse			18.9.78	(AF)[8]
Production	G-BFKW[4]	214	21.4.78	Filton			6.2.80	(BA)
Production	F-WJAN[5]	215	26.12.78	Toulouse			23.10.80	(AF)
Production	G-BFKX[6]	216	20.4.79	Filton			13.6.80	(BA)

1. The first production aircraft were retained by the manufacturers. They have been used for trials of modifications to the aircraft in service.

2. F-WTSC became F-BTSC

3. F-WJAM became F-BTSD

4. G-BFKW became G-BOAG

5. F-WJAN became F-BVFF

6. G-BFKX became G-BOAF

7. Returned to Aerospatiale 8.12.76; re-delivered AF 11.6.79

8. Returned to Aerospatiale 12.3.79; re-delivered AF 9.5.80

NOTE: Aircraft 204 to 213, and 216 (briefly), wore US registration numbers while operating between Washington and Dallas, Texas. The British registered aircraft had an abbreviated 'N' tail number inserted in place of two of their British letters – for example, G-BOAA became G-N94AA. The G was removed while they were in the USA. The French aircraft used a slightly different system: for example, F-BVFA became N94FA. In all cases the two last letters gave the clue to the real identity.

Chronology

1956

Basic supersonic airliner research starts in Britain and France.
5 November British Supersonic Transport Aircraft Committee (STAC) first meets.

1959–61

SST feasibility and design studies undertaken in Britain and France.

1961

Anglo-French discussions on commonality of SST requirements and design studies lead to investigation of possible collaboration; discussions take place between BAC and Sud Aviation in Paris and at Weybridge.

1962

29 November British and French governments sign agreement for joint design, development and manufacture of a supersonic airliner.

1963

Preliminary design for 100-seat SST discussed with key airlines.
May First metal cut for test specimens.
June First Concorde sales option signed by Pan American. Later in June, BOAC and Air France also sign Concorde sales options.

1964

May Announcement of developed aircraft (at IATA Technical Committee Meeting in Beirut) with increased wing area and lengthened fuselage, providing accommodation for up to 118 passengers – the design subsequently 'frozen' for prototype manufacture.

July Olympus 593 'D' (Derivative) engine first run at Bristol, England.

1965

April First metal cut for Concorde prototypes.
May Pre-production Concorde design (130 seats) announced.
October Prototype Concorde sub-assemblies started.
November Olympus 593 'B' (Big) engine first run at Bristol.

1966

Detailed and continuing discussions, on all aspects of Concorde development, begin between manufacturers and specialist engineering committees representing all customer airlines.

March Sixteen-ton centre fuselage/wing section for static and thermal testing delivered to CEAT, Toulouse, France.

April Final assembly of Concorde prototype 001 begins at Toulouse.

June Concorde main flight simulator commissioned at Toulouse. Complete Olympus 593 engine and variable geometry exhaust assembly first testbed run at Melun-Villaroche, France.

August Final assembly of Concorde prototype 002 begins at Filton (Bristol), England.

September Vulcan flying testbed with Olympus 593 makes first flight. Olympus 593 first run in Cell 3 high-altitude facility, NGTE Pyestock, England.

October Olympus 593 achieves 35,190 lb (dry) thrust on test at Bristol, exceeding 'Stage 1' brochure requirement.

December 70-foot-long fuselage and nose section delivered to RAE Farnborough for fatigue testing.

1967

February Full-scale Concorde interior mock-up at Filton first presented to customer airlines.

April Complete Olympus 593 engine first test-run in the high-altitude chamber at Saclay, France.

May Concorde options reach a total of 74 from 16 airlines.

August Concorde 001 undergoes resonance testing at Toulouse.

11 December First prototype Concorde 001 rolled out at Toulouse.

1968

January Vulcan flying testbed logs first 100 hours in the air. SNECMA variable-geometry exhaust assembly for Olympus 593 engine cleared at Melun-Villaroche for flight in the Concorde prototypes.

February British government announces provision of £125 million loan to launch production of aircraft and engines.

March Preliminary engine testing in Concorde 001 at Toulouse.

August First taxi trials by Concorde 001 at Toulouse.

September Second prototype Concorde 002 rolled out at Filton.

December Olympus 593 ground testing reaches 5000 hours.

1969

2 March Maiden flight of French-assembled Concorde protototype 001 at Toulouse. Later in March, governmental authority is given for a total of nine Concorde airframes – two prototypes, two pre-production, two ground test airframes, and three series production aircraft.

9 April Maiden flight of British-assembled Concorde prototype 002 from Filton to Fairford (Gloucestershire).

June Both Concorde prototypes make first public appearance at Paris Air Show.

July Annular combustion system design specified for all subsequent Concordes to remove exhaust smoke.

1 October Concorde 001 first achieves Mach 1.

8 November First airline pilots fly Concorde 001.

December Governmental authority given for three more series production Concordes – numbers 204, 205, 206.

1970

February Longest single engine test on Olympus 593. Engine ran for 300 hours – a time equivalent to nearly 100 trans-Atlantic Concorde flights.

25 March Concorde 002 first achieves Mach 1.

May New-design TRA (Thrust Reverser Aft) engine nozzle specified for improved weight, aerodynamic and noise qualities on production Concordes.

August Flights resumed with Olympus 593-3B engines and auto-controlled air intakes.

1 September Concorde 002 makes first flight on British West Coast test corridor.

13 September Concorde 002 appears at SBAC Farnborough Air Show and then makes first landing at an international airport – London Heathrow.

4 November Concorde 001 first achieves Mach 2.

12 November Concorde 002 first achieves Mach 2.

1971

January First 100 supersonic flights logged.

April Four more production Concordes (numbers 207–210) are authorized, together with approval for purchase of long-dated materials for the next six production aircraft (numbers 211–216).

13 May Concorde 001 makes first automatic landing.

25 May Concorde 001 appears at Paris Air Show and then flies to Dakar in West Africa (2500 miles) in 2 hours 7 minutes – first intercontinental flight.

June Total Concorde flight test time reaches 500 hours. Bench and flight development engine testing totals 10,000 hours.

July Airline pilots fly at Mach 2.

August Flight clearance obtained for Olympus 593-4 engine standard. First 100 bisonic flights logged.

4–18 September Concorde 001 makes trouble-free fifteen-day tour of South America.

20 September Concorde 01 – the first pre-production aircraft – rolled out at Filton.

14 December US Federal Aviation Agency announces that Concorde will be within American airport noise limits.

17 December Concorde 01 makes maiden flight from Filton to Fairford.

21 December All three flying Concordes – 001, 002 and 01 – on test flights simultaneously.

22 December Pricing formula for initial Concorde customer airlines announced in British Parliament.

1972

6 January The three Concordes together at Fairford.

7 February Concorde 002 flies with production undercarriage.

12 February Concorde 01 flies supersonic.

February Concorde 02 – the second pre-production aircraft – structurally complete at Toulouse.

March First and second series production Concordes near structural completion at Toulouse and Filton.

13 April British and French governments authorize production of further six series production Concordes (211–216) and announce Concorde 002's mission to Far East and Australia in June.

22–23 April Concorde 002 makes first appearance in Germany – at Hanover Air Show.

April Delivery of first Olympus 593 Mk. 602 to Toulouse for Concorde 02. Total Olympus 593 engine running experience exceeds 20,000 hours.

3 May Concorde 001 flies from Toulouse to Tangier.

18 May 1000 Concorde flying hours now logged by 001, 002 and 01.

25 May BOAC announces that it is to order a fleet of five Concordes.

2 June Concorde 002 leaves Fairford to begin 45,000 mile sales demonstration tour of twelve countries in the Far East and Australia.

1 July Concorde 002 returns on time to London Heathrow on completion of tour.

28 July BOAC signs contract with BAC in London for five Concordes and Air France with Aerospatiale in Paris for four Concordes. Both airlines to take delivery in 1975.

10 August Concorde 01 returns to Filton for ground programme to bring it up to near full production standard – notably the installation of Olympus 593 Mk. 602 power plants.

4–10 September Concorde 002 appears daily at the flying display at the SBAC Farnborough Show and also makes 'show the people' flights to several areas of the UK.

14 September Governmental approval given for the procurement of advance materials for six more series production Concordes (numbers 217–222).

28 September Concorde 02 – the second pre-production aircraft – rolled out at Toulouse.

11 December British government approves Bill to raise production financial loan from £125 million (see February 1968) to £350 million.

1973

10 January Concorde 02 makes maiden flight at Toulouse.

22 January Concorde 002 leaves Fairford for a two-and-a-half week period of 'hot and high' airfield performance trials at Jan Smuts Airport at Johannesburg, South Africa.

31 January Pan American and TWA decide not to take up their Concorde options.

20 February Concorde 002 successfully completes performance trials at Johannesburg and demonstrations at Cape Town.

23 February Concorde 02 makes 3728 mile (6000 km) non-stop flight from Toulouse to Iceland and return – equivalent to Paris–New York – in 3 hours 27 minutes, of which 2 hours 9 minutes at Mach 2.

24 February Concorde 002 returns to Fairford from South Africa trials.

3 March Concorde 02 makes 3900 mile (6280 km) flight from Toulouse to West Africa and return in 3 hours 38 minutes – equivalent to Frankfurt–New York.

15 March Concorde 01 returns from Filton to Fairford after major modification programme, notably the installation of production standard engine air intakes and the smoke-free Olympus 593 Mk. 602 engines as in 02.

June High-altitude sampling flights made by 001 and 002 in support of international research programmes to improve knowledge of the stratosphere.

30 June Flight from Las Palmas to Fort Lamy (Chad) for observation of solar eclipse by Concorde 001. Concorde speed gave 80 minutes of continuous observing time for the scientists on board.

9 July Concorde 002 begins three weeks of temperature and altitude accountability trials at Torrejon, near Madrid (2000 feet above sea level).

18 September Concorde 02 leaves Paris, Orly for its first visit to the USA for the opening of Dallas Fort Worth Airport. *En route*, visits Las Palmas and Caracas.

26 September Concorde returns from USA in record-breaking time of 3 hours 33 minutes non-stop from Washington to Paris.

19 October Prototype 001 is retired to French Air Museum at Le Bourget Airport after 397 flights covering 812 hours block time, 255 of which were at supersonic speeds.

6 December The first production Concorde, F-WTSB, makes its maiden flight from Toulouse. Airborne for 2 hours 40 minutes, it reaches a speed of Mach 1·57.

1974

7 February Concorde 02 flies to Fairbanks, Alaska for 'cold soak' tests at low temperatures.

13 February First flight of second production Concorde, G-BBDG. On 1 hour 45 minute flight to Fairford, reaches supersonic speeds.

19 February Concorde 02 returns after satisfactory completion of trials in Alaska.

5 June Concorde 02 makes a 12,000 mile trip from Paris to Rio de Janeiro and back in only 12 hours 47 minutes. This was the climax of a series of daily return flights between Paris and Rio de Janeiro in which the reliability of the aircraft was demonstrated.

13–18 June Two return trips Paris to Boston by Concorde 02, and short stop in Miami. On 17 June Concorde left Boston as a 747 left Paris for Boston. Concorde flew to Paris and returned to Boston before the 747 arrived.

25 June The static test specimen in Toulouse (CEAT) tested to destruction after completion of tests demonstrating the airframe's capability of withstanding the design aerodynamic and inertial load.

19 July V. Giscard d'Estaing, President of France, and Harold Wilson, Prime Minister of Britain, agree in Paris on an initial run of sixteen Concordes.

7 August Second production Concorde leaves London Heathrow for hot-weather-flight and ground-handling trials in Bahrain, visiting Teheran *en route*. (Trials successfully completed in just under three weeks.)

27 August The first of a series of demonstration flights in the Middle East with second production Concorde. Places visited: Qatar, Kuwait, Abu Dhabi, Dubai and Muscat.

3 September Second production Concorde leaves Bahrain for several days of runway response trials in Singapore before returning to Fairford.

12 September 3000 hours of flight testing achieved.

1 October Completion of cabin mock-up refurbishing with the 'new look' incorporating sculptured side-wall panels, improved lighting and enclosed overhead bins.

20–28 October Concorde 02 American Pacific coast tour covering London, Gander, Mexico City, San Francisco, Anchorage, Los Angeles, Lima, Bogota, Caracas, Las Palmas, Paris.

21 October 1000 hours supersonic flying amassed by the six Concordes.

28 October Second production Concorde based at Casablanca, Morocco, for seven weeks of certification testing. A series of take-off and noise measurements are made, as well as cold air supersonic cruise checks. First production aircraft also at Casablanca on intake control work.

7 November Concorde 01 flies to Moses Lake, USA, via Bangor, Maine, for natural de-icing trials, making fastest-ever civil crossing of the North Atlantic.

1975

29 January CIAP report, sponsored by US Department of Transportation, describes SSTs as merely a pimple on the overall environmental problem compared with other sources of pollution. The report particularly looked at the possible effect of SSTs on the upper atmosphere, in particular on the ozone layer.

31 January Third production Concorde, F-WTSC, makes its maiden flight.

11 February Completion of passenger emergency evacuation certification trials.

26 February Concorde 01 flies to Nairobi, Kenya, via Cairo, for two weeks of tropical icing trials.

27 February Supersonic maiden flight of fourth production Concorde, G-BOAC.

28 February The start of three weeks' trials for the second production Concorde at Madrid covering certification work on runway, take-off, landing and climb performance.

3 March Concorde 02 engaged on flooded runway tests for several days. Draft Environmental Impact Statement on proposed operation of Concorde into the US delivered by the FAA on the basis of two flights per day to JFK, New York, and one flight per day to Dulles, Washington, followed by public hearing.

15 April First of a series of air conditioning system flights with full passenger load.

25 April Two weeks of Air France flight-crew training at Dakar begins.

6 May France and Brazil finalize agreement permitting Air France Concorde to land in Brazil on scheduled flights.

28 May Special Category C. of A. for third production Concorde awarded by French Aviation Authority SGAC. Registration changed to F-BTSC. Start of Endurance flying by third production Concorde; routes flown are: Paris–Dakar–Paris (once); Paris–Rio, via Dakar (fifteen round trips); Paris–Caracas, via Lisbon (twelve round trips); Paris–Gander (four round trips); North Atlantic–Mediterranean (six sorties).

30 May At Paris Air Show Concorde 02 on static display. First production aircraft in flying programme.

9 June Endurance flights with first production Concorde including Keflavik, Bodo, Shannon, Tangier, Dakar and subsonic flights within France to Charles de Gaulle, Lyon, Marseilles, Lille and Nice.

19 June BA start flight training at Fairford.

30 June Special Category C. of A. was awarded to fourth production Concorde by CAA.

7 July Start of Endurance flying with fourth production Concorde. Destinations covered are: London, Bahrain, Bombay, Kuala Lumpur, Singapore, Melbourne, Beirut, Gander and Damascus.

4 October Opening of Montreal's new International Airport, Mirabel, by Concorde 02. The aircraft flies, *en route* from Paris and London, to Ottawa.

9 October French government grants the Concorde Certificate of Airworthiness No. 78.

14 October British Airways open reservations on Concorde flights to Bahrain and Air France to Rio de Janeiro, via Dakar. (Both services to start on 21 January 1976.)

25 October The fifth production Concorde (F-BVFA) makes Mach 2 maiden flight in new Air France Concorde livery.

5 November The sixth production Concorde (G-BOAA) makes Mach 2 maiden flight.

5 December British Civil Aviation Authority grant Concorde a Certificate of Airworthiness.

19 December Air France take delivery of their first Concorde – 205 (F-BVFA).

1976

6 January Air France take delivery of their second Concorde – 203 (F-BTSC).

14 January British Airways take delivery of their first Concorde – 206 (G-BOAA).

21 January Concorde into airline service simultaneously with British Airways (206, London–Bahrain), and Air France (205, Paris–Rio, via Dakar).

4 February US Secretary of Transportation, William T. Coleman, gives approval for British Airways and Air France to operate two services each per day to New York, and one service each per day to Washington for a sixteen-month trial period.

13 February British Airways take delivery of their second Concorde – 204 (G-BOAC).

4 March Concorde 002 flies to retirement in the custody of the Fleet Air Arm Museum at RNAS Yeovilton.

6 March First flight of Concorde 207, seventh production aircraft, from Toulouse.

8 April Air France take delivery of their third Concorde (F-BVFB).

9 April Air France operation extended to include once a week Concorde service to Caracas with technical stop at Santa Maria in the Azores.

18 May First flight of Concorde 208 (G-BOAB) eighth production aircraft, from Filton. 208 reached Mach 2·05 at 63,000 feet.

20 May French-assembled pre-production Concorde 02 retired to Orly Airport, Paris.

24 May British Airways and Air France start trans-Atlantic services to Washington DC.

9 July First flight of Concorde 209 (F-BVFC), ninth production aircraft, from Toulouse.

3 August Air France take delivery of their fourth Concorde (F-BVFC).

25 August First flight of Concorde 210 (G-BOAD), tenth production aircraft, from Filton.

30 September British Airways take delivery of their third Concorde – 208 (G-BOAB).

2 November Concorde 203 starts a 30,000-mile Far East demonstration tour. Starting from Paris the aircraft visits Bahrain, Singapore, Manila, Hong Kong, Djakarta and Seoul, returning to London.

30 November Fairford Flight Test Base closed and team return to Filton.

6 December British Airways take delivery of their fourth Concorde – 210 (G-BOAD).

8 December Concorde 203 returned by Air France to Aerospatiale.

1977

21 January One year in service – over 45,000 revenue passengers carried nearly three-and-a-half million miles.

10 February First flight of Concorde 211 (F-BVFD) from Toulouse. Interchange agreements filed by Braniff International for approval by US Civil Aeronautics Board to allow the airline to operate six days a week between Dallas and Washington DC using BA and AF aircraft.

17 March First flight of Concorde 212 (G-BOAE), twelfth production aircraft, from Filton.

26 March Air France take delivery of Concorde 211 (F-BVFD). This maintains their fleet of four aircraft, having returned 203 (F-BTSC) to Aerospatiale.

20 July British Airways take delivery of their fifth Concorde – 212 (G-BOAE).

20 August British-assembled pre-production Concorde 01 is retired to Duxford under care of Duxford Aviation Society.

19 October First Concorde landing in New York when 201 arrived from Toulouse for a series of proving flights.

26 October Singapore Airlines announce agreement with British Airways to operate jointly between London and Singapore via Bahrain – initially three return services a week.

22 November Inauguration of British Airways and Air France Concorde services to New York.

9 December Inauguration of British Airways/Singapore Airlines Concorde service between London and Singapore via Bahrain. Stopped after three return flights, for discussions with Malaysian government on overflying rights.

1978

21 January Two years in service, 129,000 passengers carried.

21 April First flight of Concorde 214 (G-BFKW) from Filton.

26 June First flight of Concorde 213 (F-WJAM) from Toulouse.

10 August British Airways carry their 100,000th passenger on Concorde.

1 September British Airways and Air France Concordes cleared for Category III automatic landings in poor visibility down to 250 metres visual range at 15 feet above the runway.

18 September Air France take delivery of Concorde 213 (F-WJAM).

20 September Air France open twice weekly services between Paris and Mexico City, via Washington DC.

21 November One year of service to New York. FAA monitoring report finds Concorde noise in line with or less than predicted in Environmental Impact Statement issued in November 1975.

10 December Concorde G-BOAA arrives at Dallas–Fort Worth Airport to begin proving flights to sixteen south-east and mid-American cities.
26 December First flight of Concorde 215 (F-WJAN) from Toulouse.

1979

9 January Concorde awarded United States type certificate of airworthiness.
12 January Inauguration of Braniff Concorde flights from Washington to Dallas through interchange agreement with British Airways and Air France.
21 January Three years of airline service, close to 300,000 passengers carried, and nine Concordes in service accumulate 21,700 flying hours.
24 January Re-commencement of joint BA/Singapore Airlines service between London and Singapore.
20 April The sixteenth production Concorde 216 (G-BFKX) makes a supersonic maiden flight from Filton.

1980

21 January The fourth anniversary of Concorde's commercial debut.
6 February British Airways take delivery of their sixth Concorde – 214 (G-BFKW).
13 June British Airways take delivery of their seventh Concorde — 216 (G-BFKX).
17 June Flights to Dallas by BA and AF cease.
23 October Air France take delivery of Concorde 215 (F-WJAN).
1 November Flights to Bahrain and Singapore by BA cease.

1981

21 January Five years in service.
24 May The fifth anniversary of the first supersonic commercial flight to the USA.

1982

31 March Air France cease operations to Caracas and Rio.

1984

27 March British Airways opens route to Miami *via* Washington.

1985

25 April British Airways introduces new interior furnishings and exterior livery.

1986

31 January Celebration of the tenth anniversary of commercial services by Concorde.

Index

NOTE: Technical terms (printed in small capitals) are included in this index for the purpose of definition alone. Where such a term is defined in the text, only the page reference for that definition is given. Other technical terms mentioned but not explained in the text are defined here.